Pancho Villa's Saddle at the Cadillac Bar

PANCHO VILLA'S SADDLE

at the Cadillac Bar

RECIPES AND MEMORIES

WANDA GARNER CASH

TEXAS A&M UNIVERSITY PRESS ❦ COLLEGE STATION

LIBRARY OF CONGRESS CATALOGING-IN-PUBLICATION DATA

Names: Cash, Wanda Garner, author.

Title: Pancho Villa's saddle at the Cadillac Bar : recipes and memories /
Wanda Garner Cash.

Description: First edition. | College Station, [Texas] : Texas A&M
University Press, [2020] | Includes index.

Identifiers: LCCN 2020011877 | ISBN 9781623498986 (cloth) |
ISBN 9781623498993 (ebook)

Subjects: LCSH: Bessan, Mayo, 1885–1970. | Garner, Porter S, Jr.,
1923–2007. | Cadillac Bar (Nuevo Laredo, Mexico) |
Restaurateurs—Mexico—Nuevo Laredo—Biography. | Bars (Drinking
establishments)—Mexico—Nuevo Laredo—History. |
Restaurants—Mexico—Nuevo Laredo—History. | Bartending—Mexico—Nuevo
Laredo—Anecdotes. | Restaurant management—Mexico—Nuevo
Laredo—Anecdotes. | Cooking, Cajun. | Cooking, American—Louisiana
style. | Mexican American cooking. | Nuevo Laredo (Mexico)—Social life
and customs—20th century. | Laredo (Tex.)—Social life and
customs—20th century. | LCGFT: Biographies. | Oral histories.

Classification: LCC TX950.5.A1 C37 2020 | DDC 641.87/4097212—dc23

LC record available at https://lccn.loc.gov/2020011877

CONTENTS

The pre-flood front door of the Cadillac Bar, 1953.

PREFACE

Children clambered onto Pancho Villa's saddle at Nuevo Laredo's Cadillac Bar, posing with toy six-shooters and grinning into the camera. Pretending to be cowboys or outlaws kept them busy while their parents indulged in a Ramos gin fizz or a plate of chicken envueltos.

The story of the Cadillac Bar is a love story, and a tale about women who got tipsy and danced on the bar. A beer-drinking bear. Wildcatters and vote-seeking politicians, and loyal customers who clamored for fancy drinks and New Orleans seafood.

They're all here in this oral history of the iconic institution in Nuevo Laredo, Mexico. A fabled kitchen and watering hole and its evolution from Prohibition-era New Orleans to the dusty streets of a border town into a landmark that's now only a memory for generations of customers who lingered over forty-cent tequila sours and Creole cuisine.

That fun was put on hold for almost a year in the summer of 1954, when a catastrophic flood swept away the ornate leather saddle bedecked with sterling silver fittings. After rising ten feet inside the main dining room, the floodwaters plastered everything with a stinking muck.

Pancho Villa's saddle was lost.

The Cadillac Bar was in ruins, devastating the two men whose lives were intertwined with that landmark.

Founded by Mayo Bessan in 1924, the Cadillac was destroyed and rebuilt after the 1954 flood devastated cities on both sides of the Rio Grande. Its restoration lasted almost a year before it reopened, with that midcentury engineering marvel: central air conditioning.

This is the oral history of "los dos Laredos" and the two men who endured that flood, Bessan and Porter S. Garner Jr. They lived on both sides of the Rio Grande, in Laredo, Texas, and Nuevo Laredo, Mexico. They built a dirt-floored saloon into the Cadillac Bar, an oasis attracting ranchers and lawmakers, housewives and tourists, which branched into franchises across the United States until Mexico's economic and political instability caused my family to hand over the keys to the waiters in 1979 and walk away.

The story starts in 1921, when Mayo Bessan left his job at the St. Charles Hotel in New Orleans after Prohibition turned bartending into a criminal act. Four years later, with his twenty-year-old Cajun bride in tow, he settled in the sleepy Mexican frontier town of Nuevo Laredo and opened a bar on the unpaved main street, which would eventually become part of the Pan-American Highway.

Mayo's son-in-law, Porter Garner, was an Aggie who left Texas A&M in his sophomore year for military service in World War II, which left him paralyzed in a body cast for almost a year. After Porter recovered from the injuries that left him with spinal damage and a permanent limp, he went to work at the Cadillac in 1947, not long after he married Mayo's only child, Wanda.

Mayo was my grandfather, and Porter was my dad.

I grew up behind the bar as I tagged along with them: first child and first grandchild. I spoke Spanish before I spoke English. I learned my numbers counting coins at my grandfather's desk in the kitchen office at the Cadillac. I rode Pancho Villa's saddle on a sawhorse in the main dining room, with a toy six-shooter in my holster. I fed the monkeys and parrots my grandfather kept in the Cadillac's parking lot.

On busy weekends, when tourists thronged five deep at the fifty-foot bar, I waited for a table like everybody else in the line that snaked out the door and around the corner.

December 2019 marked forty years since my father walked away from the Cadillac Bar, the landmark that stamped an indelible mark not just on him but also on our family, on its customers, and on the culture and history of the sister cities on both sides of the Rio Grande.

In this memoir, you'll meet some of the characters who were part of the Cadillac's history and hear their reminiscences in their own words. I hope you will enjoy the stories and the photographs and savor the recipes.

¡Saludos!

GRATEFUL ACKNOWLEDGMENTS

My parents, Wanda Bessan Garner and Porter S. Garner Jr.; my sister, Clay Garner Berry; and my husband, Richard Cash were my greatest inspirations for this project. Their encouragement and patience buoyed me when I didn't have the *ganas* or motivation to keep going. After my father died in 2007 and as my mother sank into the cruel fog of Alzheimer's, dying from its complications in 2010, I put the book aside until finding new inspiration when I retired from the University of Texas in 2016.

Years before that, when I began reporting for this book, I used primary sources: people who knew and loved the Cadillac Bar. People I knew personally. People who were friends of friends. People who posted on message boards and blogs and social media. Strangers.

Muchas gracias to those who contributed directly to the oral history: Jean Claire Garner Turcotte, Suzy Mayo, Jack Suneson, Russell Deutsch, Bill Mayo, Steven Levy, Gayle Ross DeGeurin, Mike DeGeurin, Michael DeGeurin, Linda Bruni, George O. Jackson, Joe Finley, Will and Pam Harte, Chula Ross Sanchez, Hector Gutierrez, Randy Matson, Sara Puig Laas, Biddy Harte Owen, Joe Phillips, Tony Proffitt, Epitacio Resendez V, Ramón and Maria Eugenia Salido, Ernie Stromberger, and Matt Sjoberg.

On Facebook and Laredo message boards, I gleaned great quotes from the following folks: Penny Gallahan Cornelius, Tom Deliganis Jr., Andy Gault, Jason L. Kuenstler, and Lynn Pugh Remadna.

Secondary sources included Jerry Thompson's "Laredo, A Pictorial History"; Maria Eugenia Guerra's "Historic Laredo: An

Illustrated History of Laredo & Webb County"; John MacCormack, writing in the San Antonio Express-News; Hugh Fitzsimons, writing in Texas Monthly; Helen Redmond, in "The Political Economy of Mexico's Drug Wars"; Mary Beth Sheridan, writing in The Seattle Times; the City of Laredo website; Webb County Historical Association; Webb County Heritage Commission; and "History of the Washington Birthday Celebration."

The following friends graciously shared their family photos: Jean Claire Garner Turcotte, Jack Suneson, John Avant, Linda and Buddy Bruni, Billy Gibbons, Will Harte, Lee Keithley Adami, Fairris Jacaman, Armando X. Lopez, Martha Hall Riklin and Melle Hall Farrell, Patty and Rocky Bruni, Glen Jackson, Janice Fitzgibbon, Bill Mayo, Steve Mims, Epitacio Resendez V, and Chula Ross Sanchez.

Thanks also to Renee LaPerriere of the Laredo Public Library, for access to the "Rescuing Texas History, 2006" and to the Portal to Texas History digital repository at the University of North Texas.

Pancho Villa's Saddle at the Cadillac Bar

⇒ 1 ⇐

Mayo

To tell the story of the Cadillac Bar, you have to tell the story of Mayo Bessan. He was a smart man and a hard drinker, and he was solely responsible for making the Cadillac what it was.

—PORTER GARNER JR., 2007

Achille Mehault "Mayo" Bessan was born January 23, 1885, in New Iberia, Louisiana, in a two-story clapboard house on Julia Street. He was part of a merged family and had some much-older half brothers and sisters.

Mostly he was raised by his oldest sister, Celestine, known as Na-Nan.

I knew many of my grandfather's cousins, but only two of his siblings: his only "full" brother, Henry, and his youngest sister, Zelime.

Henry Bessan, who was exposed to mustard gas in World War I, never married, preferring to spend time with his gambling buddies and his fighting cocks and pit bulls. He lived with Zelime and her husband, René Goulas, and their daughter, Rita, in Lafayette, Louisiana, in a rambling three-story house raised about five feet above the ground. That tight group was Mayo's closest family.

The cousins mostly lived in Abbeville, where Mayo's niece Lillian married Polycarp Broussard, had two sons, and then swathed herself in lacy peignoirs and retired to her bedroom for the rest of her life, spoiled and pampered by black servants who brought her meals and cold Coca-Colas.

During my childhood, my summer vacations always included a trip to southern Louisiana, including Abbeville, where the highlight was a trek to devour crabs and shrimp at the family fishing camp at Cypremort Point. Broussards abounded, but they never figured large in our family story.

Food was always the central character in our Louisiana trips and our family life.

My maternal grandmother, Odette Savoie Bessan, set the itinerary. Although she didn't get her driver's license until she was almost fifty years old, she was the navigator in the family. First we would head east on US 90 to New Orleans, where my great-grandfather Clay Savoie had a general store in the Westwego suburb, and in later years, to New Iberia, where he lived on a pecan orchard on Spanish Lake.

"Granpa's" wife died young, in 1946, soon after my parents married. From then on, Clay Savoie lived with his wife's unmarried sister, Edna Martin. For thirty years they took care of each other like loving, if quarrelsome, siblings.

Granpá's home was a spoiled child's paradise. He called me *pauvre bête* or *cher ti bête*, depending on how foolishly or endearingly I behaved.

Mornings, we wandered in his vast garden, pinching green beans and okra for snacks, gathering brown eggs from his speckled Dominickers, our noses bewitched by sweet gardenia bushes and loamy earth. Back at the house, Aunt Edna had only to open the back door to entice us home with the aromas of onions and bell peppers sautéing in oil and just-boiled shrimp dusted with cayenne.

It was the kind of summer idyll that I tried to bequeath to my two sons when we moved to the Hill Country in 1980, to a family compound of grandparents, great-grandparents, vegetable gardens, peacocks, and air scented with honeysuckle, mountain laurel, and the Guadalupe River.

If Granpá's house on Spanish Lake, just outside New Iberia, was a leafy retreat, entering the Lafayette relatives' house was stepping into another age, where my great-aunt Zelime presided in frilly bed jackets and Uncle Henry slept until noon and cared for the fancy roosters he had raised since childhood.

The house exuded the swampy mustiness of old people, old clothes, and uncomfortable horsehair furniture. In the evening, while the adults focused on their highballs, cheese straws, and jokes, the only ones paying attention to me were their house-keepers, Ti Lute and Arizona, whose last names I never knew.

Uncle Henry was a resourceful storyteller, and from him I learned what little I knew about the early history of my grand-father, "Big Daddy" Mayo Bessan.

My favorite story was that Mayo refused to be weaned from his mother's breast, so he nursed the family's nanny goat until he was about nine years old. At least, according to Uncle Henry.

After a brief career as an altar boy, Mayo grew up fast, sup-porting himself by gambling at cards and staging cockfights with Henry's roosters.

At the turn of the century, not much was happening in New Ibe-ria, and what jobs there were involved working for the McIlhenny

Mayo and his buddies at a picnic lunch in New Iberia, circa 1920.

family, who produced Tabasco at their plantation on nearby Avery Island. But Mayo wasn't about to go to work for the boys he regularly bested at euchre and poker.

Ninety miles east, New Orleans beckoned, with never-ending card games and fancy drinks.

In 1903, that's where Mayo headed, playing poker and tending bar in the "Tenderloin District." For a while, Mayo worked for one of his brothers-in-law as a waiter and bartender at the St. Charles Hotel. He also mixed drinks and ran card games at other popular watering holes, such as Fabacher's original bar and, later, the Rathskeller, Gluck's, Galatoire's, and the Cosmopolitan Hotel.

Porter: *It was the New Orleans of Jelly Roll Morton and Papa Celestin and his Original Tuxedo Jazz Orchestra. All the national headliners*

Always a dapper dresser, Mayo poses here with his dog Jack in New Orleans in 1922.

came to New Orleans—heavyweight champion Jess Willard and a young Sophie Tucker. Mayo worked at the greatest bars of them all, Mr. Carl Ramos's famous Imperial Cabinet, and later, the Stag. My father-in-law couldn't have had a better school for the Cadillac Bar than the New Orleans of that day.

After being stabbed in a bar fight, Mayo was sidelined by surgery and a long recovery. But what really ran him out of New Orleans was the onset of Prohibition in 1920. Mayo, then thirty-five years old, went back to New Iberia, moved into the Hotel Frederic, and set up bachelor housekeeping.

Porter: *Mayo was looking around for something to do, and he bought or leased kind of a newsstand deal. It was not just a kiosk. It was a real store. And in the back, he had a poker game going most of the time. He was a helluva card player, and that was his livelihood.*

Quite a number of people played in the game, including that guy [David] Weeks, who owned the Shadows plantation on the Bayou Teche.

One day a guy walked into the store and wrote a note to the clerk behind the counter, "Where's the action in this town?" The fellow was a deaf-mute, and he communicated by writing notes.

Mayo said, "Okay, let him in." Soon the stranger started beating the socks off the regular poker players. After a while they got tired of this, so they ganged up on him and started cheating by mumbling to each other what cards they were holding. But because he was such a nice guy, their consciences got the best of them, so they stopped.

When it came time for him to leave town, the poker players went to the train station to say farewell to him and his winnings. So he's standing at the observation deck waving goodbye. As the train pulls out, the deaf stranger yells, "Goodbye, Shorty!" to one of Mayo's friends. He really cleaned 'em out.

In New Iberia, the Savoie and Bessan families knew each other in that unavoidable small-town way where no secrets last beyond the first whispered promise.

When he wasn't playing cards, Mayo would watch Odette

Savoie walking past the store on her way to and from high school. He was about twenty years older than Odette, the same age as her father.

Odette was born July 24, 1905. Mayo said he fell in love with Odette when she was a little girl and told people he was going to marry her.

When Odette graduated from high school, Mayo finally proposed. Odette's father wasn't too happy about her marrying an older man, especially a gambler without a regular job. Eventually Mayo and Clay Savoie became great friends.

Odette and Mayo married in July 1923. He gave her a pearl necklace before they headed to Texas on their honeymoon.

Porter: *When Mayo and Odette got married, she had just turned eighteen, and he was almost forty. They went to San Antonio for their honeymoon and stayed with Mayo's cousin, Tony Bessan, who owned a radio station.*

Mayo told Odette, "You know, since we're this close, I think I'll run down to Mexico for a few days."

If you had known them, you would realize it wasn't that big of a deal to leave his bride on their honeymoon. Mayo always treated her like a daughter, took care of her, and told her what to do.

Mayo took the train to Nuevo Laredo and spent a few days looking at the possibilities of life and livelihood in a wide-open border town. Pancho Villa had just been caught and killed in Parral.

The first international bridge had been built across the Rio Grande in 1922. The country was peaceful; liquor was cheap and so was rent. Business was booming on both sides of the border.

What he saw on his 1923 visit to Laredo and Nuevo Laredo was a rough culture in comparison to the relative gentility of New Orleans and southern Louisiana.

Borderland bars were stark, dim-lit places, often with dirt floors, where the alcohol options were cheap beer and gullet-burning mescal.

To Mayo, it was the Promised Land.

Soon he would be serving these same customers fancy drinks

with names they'd never heard and ingredients they didn't know existed.

Courtney Bond, writing about the Cadillac and the Ramos gin fizz in the *Texas Monthly* in 2015, said Mayo gave Prohibition "the one-fingered salute and decamped for Mexico with Ramos's recipe."

Porter: *After about a week, Mayo returned to San Antonio, gathered up his bride, and took the Sunset Limited back to New Iberia. Not much later, he left Odette with her parents and went back to Nuevo Laredo and worked as a bartender at the Club Bar. It was owned by Nick Baccaro, who also owned the Bohemian Club, which later became known as the C.O.D.*

The whole time he worked at the Bohemian Club, Mayo had his eye on a little bar across the street, property owned by Memo Salinas-Puga's father. This was the property that eventually became Marti's.

After his bartending stint in Nuevo Laredo, Mayo went home to Odette in New Iberia, convinced that their future lay in that foreign place. To Mayo, who spoke English and French, Spanish didn't seem much of a barrier.

Porter: *Soon a Mexican friend wired him that the Salinas property was available, so Mayo made a deal to lease the building. That was the first "little" Cadillac Bar. He called it the Cadillac because [the name] sounded rich.*

Mayo and Odette moved to Nuevo Laredo in early 1924. The Bessans lived on the Mexican side of the Rio Grande for about two years, until a few months after their only child, Wanda Mae, was born in 1926.

Odette didn't speak Spanish and had few friends. Left mostly on her own in a strange country where the food and the people were as unfamiliar as the language, my grandmother told me she cried every day for almost a year. She was homesick, lonely, and afraid.

Mayo posed for this picture in front of Martin High School in Laredo in 1925, shortly after moving to the border city.

Mayo and Odette's neighbors on Victoria Street were Don Octaviano Longoria and his wife, Sara Theriot, whose family had followed a similar path after the Civil War, from New Orleans to Texas to Mexico.

The Longorias had a grocery store and eight children. Their oldest son, Chito, who was the same age as Odette, grew the family business into a Mexican empire, Industrias Unidas, that made a fortune in commodities trading during World War II. Chito Longoria later became the Cadillac's landlord.

Sara Theriot Longoria was kind to Odette, speaking to her in French and teaching her Spanish, helping her cope with the mysteries of living in Mexico.

Years later, when Odette and Mayo lived on Aldama Street in the Montrose district of Laredo, the Longorias' daughter, Lilia, and her husband, Ernest Bruni, lived nearby on Market Street. Ernest and Mayo were close friends, and Ernest was a regular customer at the Cadillac. The Brunis' son, Buddy, and daughter, Evelyn, were Wanda's younger playmates.

Odette never demanded much from Mayo, but on one issue she was firm. She refused to deliver her baby in Mexico. That probably was the right emotional—and perhaps medical—decision, but it surely was shortsighted considering the potential of future citizenship and ownership of the family business.

Mayo complied. Wanda Mae was born in Laredo's Mercy Hospital, but her first home was in Nuevo Laredo in the little apartment on Victoria Street, just down the street from the Cadillac.

While Wanda Mae was still a baby, Mayo and Odette moved to Laredo, to a little house on Zaragoza Street near San Agustín Church, in the area where La Posada Hotel now stands. This neighborhood, La Azteca, is one of Laredo's oldest, where a few graceful sandstone houses survive, with their dry-stacked arches and cypress lintels.

The Bessans rented the house from the Rodriguezes, who befriended the couple and adopted Mayo, Odette, and baby Wanda Mae into their family.

In their first home, the Bessans had a courtyard with fragrant lime and orange trees. When Odette and the baby sat on the patio in the evening while Mayo was across the river at work, they breathed in the familiar Laredo perfume: an exotic mix of citrus blossoms, pungent chili piquins, and the sweet smell of wet dirt, as the neighbor women sprayed the street with water hoses to keep the dust down.

Odette Bessan and Wanda Mae, 1926, Nuevo Laredo.

When Wanda Mae was four or five, the Bessans moved to Victoria Street, where their neighbors were the Peter Leyendeckers and the Alexanders. Wanda's earliest playmate was Roslyn Alexander, daughter of rancher and banker Ben Alexander, who headed the Laredo National Bank. Roslyn later married Max Mandel, who succeeded his father-in-law at the bank.

This was known as St. Peter's neighborhood, after the first English-speaking Catholic church in Laredo. According to Jerry Thompson's history of Laredo, the area was sometimes called the depot district because of its proximity to the passenger station of the International and Great Northern Railroad.

The neighborhood developed between 1881 and World War I, as European and Jewish immigrants settled in Laredo, many of whom became Laredo's most prominent citizens. The tumultuous Mexican Revolution of 1910–1920 also washed a tide of immigrants to Laredo. Many found work in the booming fields of coal mining, onion cultivation, and brick manufacturing, and later in oil and gas production across Webb County and in neighboring Mirando City.

The 1920s brought new prosperity, economic growth, and modernization to the two Laredos. On the American side, downtown streets were being paved, and the venerable Hamilton Hotel grew from three stories to eleven. In 1922, Nuevo Laredo was the port of entry for 70 percent of US exports to Mexico.

Forty years later, the first foreign-owned manufacturing plant in Mexico, a maquiladora, was built in Nuevo Laredo, heralding an era of intense industrialization.

But in 1924, the bridge to Nuevo Laredo had been reopened for only a short time, rebuilt after a fire three years earlier. Before the formal structures, people relied on a ferry to carry them back and forth across the Rio Grande. The ferry crossing was at Water Street and Flores Avenue, Laredo's main business area in the late nineteenth century. Before a foot-and-wagon bridge was built in 1889, people in Los Dos Laredos used the *chalanes*, pole-driven ferries, to cross the river.

A history of Laredo on the city's website says that location has been a well-known point for crossing the Rio Grande, first noted in

1745 by explorer Jacinto de León, who identified it as the Paso de los Indios, an old Indian crossing. The city's website says the river "provided a way of life for the settlers, as river perch became part of the Spanish settlers' diet, crops planted in the fertile river valley provided an abundant harvest, and *carrizo,* cane, was used as thatch for their hut-like homes called *jacales.* The steep banks of the river were rich with sandstone, lime, and mud, durable materials that contributed to the border's unique architectural legacy."

Don Tomás Sánchez, the founder of Laredo, chose the site of the new town because of the favorable river crossing. The original 1755 settlement was first called Villa de San Agustín de Laredo, after a town in Spain.

In 1839, after almost a century as a corridor to the interior of Mexico and general neglect by the governments in both Mexico and the United States, residents of the area formed a government of their own, the Republic of the Rio Grande, with Laredo as its capital.

Though the republic lasted only about ten months, the tenure makes Laredo unique among Texas towns, having endured under seven flags, instead of the six claimed by the Lone Star State.

Following the 1848 Treaty of Guadalupe Hidalgo, residents living north of the Rio Grande became American citizens, while those who wanted to remain Mexican citizens moved across the river and established Nuevo (new) Laredo.

During most of the Cadillac's heyday, Laredo had only one bridge into Mexico. Today there are five bridges; Laredo is the leading port of entry into Mexico and Central and South America.

But before Amistad Dam was built upriver, in Del Rio in 1969, Laredo and Nuevo Laredo endured regular flooding from the wild Rio Grande. Bridges were washed out and then quickly rebuilt to handle the increasing traffic.

In 1924, Nuevo Laredo was a scrappy border town with a population of about 15,000. The primary form of transportation was horse and buggy. Cars were rare on both sides of the river, but Laredo did have a country club, and an electric streetcar line that operated until 1937.

Alcohol was big business, too. With the advent of Prohibition,

D&M Distributors moved its distillery from Kentucky to Ciudad Juárez in 1922.

When Mayo arrived in Nuevo Laredo, all it took for an American to immigrate to Mexico was to sign papers at the *aduana* (customs), declaring yourself a resident alien. You got an *inmigrante* permit, and after five renewals you were an *inmigrado*, a permanent immigrant with all the rights of a citizen, except for voting and property ownership within twenty miles of the border.

Mayo completed the paperwork and obtained dual citizenship for himself, but Odette chose not to officially immigrate. Some twenty years later, Porter followed suit, eventually obtaining dual citizenship.

Laredo's economy was driven by three "booms"—agriculture (primarily onions), oil and gas, and commerce—on the Pan-American Highway, which stretches from Canada to Panama.

The river itself has always connected people living on each side. Families have straddled the Rio Grande since the 1848 Treaty of Guadalupe Hidalgo divided the territory between Texas and Mexico. Nuevo Laredo was founded that same year when a handful of families settled on the Mexican side, preferring to remain Mexican. Folklore has it that they took the bones of their ancestors with them so they could have eternal rest in Mexican ground.

During the early years of the Cadillac, Mayo imported Louisiana friends to help him run the place and establish the "We are from New Orleans" ambience at the bar and in the kitchen. These included New Orleans–trained bartenders: Nat Dupuis, Al Roschuni, Pat Perry, Dominic Bonin, and Mayo's brother-in-law, Andrew Buillard. Mayo always formally addressed him as Mr. Buillard, or used his nickname John L., because of his resemblance to the prizefighter John L. Sullivan.

As a side enterprise, the Louisiana crew organized a gambling operation in the back room: poker, craps, roulette tables, and slot machines. "That's when he really started making money," my mother said.

The gambling ended in 1935 during the tenure of Mexican president Lázaro Cárdenas, but Mayo kept the slot machines and hoped the government wouldn't notice.

Wanda Bessan Garner: *One of my early memories of the Cadillac was the back room for gambling. Every Saturday my father would come home for lunch and take me back with him in the afternoon. He'd give me a handful of coins, and I'd stand on a chair and play the slots.*

About sixty old slot machines in the parking lot storeroom were lost in the flood.

Mr. Buillard and his wife, Mayo's older sister Na-Nan, lived with Mayo and Odette for about a year in the St. Peter's neighborhood. My grandmother always said that Na-Nan saved her life in what she still regarded as a foreign, hostile place.

Mayo's main ally and nemesis at the Cadillac was Al Roschuni, a burly man whose girth matched his height. Mayo knew Al from New Orleans, where the two of them had tended bar in nearly all the same famous places. Al also was a manager of Childs Restaurant, a famous chain of eateries at the turn of the twentieth century.

Al loved sports and boxing, and by all accounts was a fair baseball player. He was an adventurer and storyteller and claimed to have been the timekeeper in the prizefight in Havana in 1915, when Jack Johnson beat "the great white hope" Jess Willard.

On his first visit to Nuevo Laredo, Al was dodging bootlegging charges in New Orleans. Mayo's version of the story recounted how Al and a friend who owned a boat were running rum from Cuba to New Orleans. One night, with the boat's hold full of illegal liquor, the captain unknowingly tied up next to a Coast Guard cutter.

One step ahead of the revenuers, Al telegraphed Mayo asking for train fare and a job. During their twenty-five-year association at the Cadillac, Mayo and Al feuded over recipes, money, and cards. They loved and respected each other, but they quarreled most of the time. After Al died, Mayo liked to recall that Al either quit or was fired a dozen times.

With the Cadillac's fancy drinks and a kitchen that turned out broiled seafood and delicate sauces, things were rocking along in Mexico, in spite of Prohibition and the impending Great Depression in the United States.

Then the Mexican government began its stretch of the Pan-American Highway, which would eventually travel from the Panama Canal to the Canadian border.

When construction reached Nuevo Laredo in 1929, Mexico decreed that no liquor would be served within ten meters of the highway. The distance was such that Mayo's "little" Cadillac would be reduced to about eight feet of space.

Undaunted, he started looking for another location.

A couple of blocks away, at the corner of Belden and Ocampo, was the site of a former bar called the Caballo Blanco, which had been operated by Mauro Cipriano. It was vacant at the time, owned by the Benavides, a Texas ranching family of Mexican descent.

Mayo made a deal to rent the building. At midnight, July 3, 1929, he closed the Guerrero Street bar and opened in the new location at ten a.m. the next day. He never missed a drink order.

When the Depression hit Texas about 1930, Mexico, like much of the world economies, experienced its own recession, especially in agriculture.

Porter: *The worst year in Texas was 1932. One day Pete Coussoulis, who ran the Cadillac's kitchen, was griping about the economy.*

A promotional photo of Mayo's Cadillac Bar, 1929.

Mayo, left, with Nat Dupuis and his brother-in-law Andrew "John
L." Buillard at the "big" Cadillac at the corner of Belden and
Ocampo in 1929. Buillard was nicknamed John L., in reference to
his resemblance to John L. Sullivan. He was married to Celestine Bessan, Mayo's oldest sister, who raised him. Mr. Buillard
worked at the Cadillac, while Celestine, who was known as Na-
Nan, helped Odette with Wanda.

*Mayo asked him how much he had in the kitchen operation, and
Mayo bought him out on the spot. From then on, it was all Mayo's.
Pete later owned the Southland Café in downtown Laredo.*

During the economic downturn in Mexico, places like the Cadillac relied on American customers, neighbors from Laredo and San
Antonio, Mirando City, Cotulla, and Hebbronville: ranchers and oil-
men who liked good food and good drinks. Even so, times were
tough in America.

⇒ 2 ⇐

Porter Joins the Business

In 1947, my father, Porter Garner, was working for his father's best friend, Johnny Ward, selling insurance. He and my mother were living in a rent house on Malinche Street, catercorner from Mayo and Odette's house on Aldama.

My father was still recovering from near-fatal injuries he suffered in Germany in World War II. On April 11, 1945, a German artillery shell exploded about ten yards away from him. The shrapnel broke his right shoulder and arm and sliced into his chest and

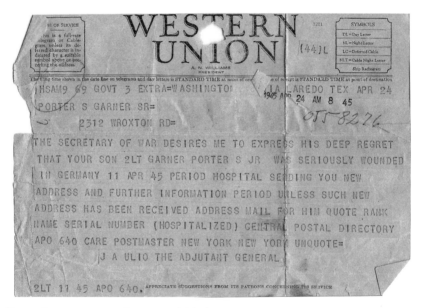

Porter's war injury telegram, 1945. Army doctors told my grandparents Porter would never walk again, but he proved them wrong.

spine, paralyzing him. Army doctors told my grandparents he would never walk again.

Writing with his left hand—scribbling, really—Porter wrote his father from a British hospital, imploring him not tell his mother how "bad it is. I am only telling you, Dad, so you'll know if something goes wrong."

After the lengthy hospitalization in England, Porter was transferred to the Percy Jones Army Hospital in Battle Creek, Michigan. From Laredo, Texas, Michigan seemed as far away as England.

My grandfather, Porter Sr., called his old friend Lyndon Baines Johnson, who was then a US congressman. Porter Sr. had known

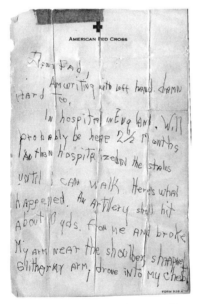
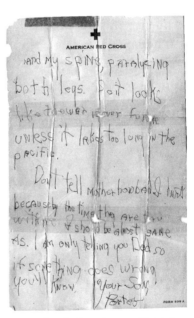

Scribbling with his left hand, Porter wrote his father from a British hospital and implored him not tell his mother about the severity of his injury. "I am only telling you, Dad, so you'll know if something goes wrong." Porter suffered wounds that keep him hospitalized in a full body cast for almost twelve months. After being treated in England immediately after the injury, the Garners got word his stateside treatment would continue at Percy Jones Army Hospital in Michigan. Porter Sr. called his old friend Congressman Lyndon Johnson, who interceded and got the medical orders changed to McCloskey General Hospital in Temple, Texas.

Johnson when he was a legislative aide to congressman Richard Kleberg and my grandfather was superintendent of schools in Riviera and Robstown.

Johnson pulled the right strings and arranged for Porter Jr. to be sent instead to McCloskey General Hospital in Temple.

My father spent about nine months in a body cast, but he proved the doctors wrong, climbing into boats and deer stands and playing golf for decades, not to mention meeting the demands at the Cadillac, and his 12th Man duties at A&M, standing up during years of Aggie football games.

Two years after his injuries, Porter was still limping and dragging one leg. But he didn't talk about it, then or ever, until I prodded him for this book.

Jim Mayo, who became my father's best friend, had been stationed at the Laredo army base as a pilot and gunnery school

The Mayos and the Garners enjoyed a rare couple's friendship spanning almost seventy years. Here they enjoy another rarity. Porter got to sit down for dinner with them on a Saturday night at the Cadillac in 1959.

instructor. Over their forty-year-friendship, Jim knew firsthand Porter's determination to overcome his disabilities.

Jim, from Tulsa, Oklahoma, married Suzy Neel in Laredo in 1943. Suzy, my "other mother," died in 2018, just shy of her ninety-fifth birthday. Jim died in 1979.

Suzy Mayo: *After Jim left the Army Air Corps, we decided to stay in Laredo and buy Harry Fansler's mapping company. The office was downtown, next to the Sames-Moore Building, where Johnny Ward had his insurance agency and Porter worked.*

Jim asked Porter to play golf with him, and Porter kept begging off, saying it was a ridiculous suggestion considering his disability. Porter finally agreed, but he told Jim if he fell down and needed help getting up, he'd ask for it. After their first game, Jim said he felt so bad because Porter had grass burs in his hair and in his socks. He said Porter had fallen down so many times, he just knew Porter would never play with him again. But he did, and, after a while, Porter didn't fall down so much. Later, Jim said he regretted giving Porter strokes.

One evening after dinner, in the spring of 1947, Mayo showed up at my parents' little rent house and made small talk for a few minutes. Then he said Al Roschuni was sick and had to quit working, and that if my father wouldn't come work with him at the Cadillac, he was going to close the place.

Porter: *I didn't speak a word of Spanish, and I didn't know anything about the business or working in Mexico. I asked Johnny Ward for advice. Johnny said it would be a wonderful opportunity if I would always remember one*

Porter behind the bar in 1952.

thing: stay on the right side of the bar. I took him at his word, and the entire time I worked at the Cadillac, I never had one drink when we were open for business. There was no way I could drink with one person and not another.

Porter acquired a reputation as a genial host, greeting customers by name, even if it had been years between visits. With his arrival, the geographical heart of the Cadillac shifted from southern Louisiana to College Station, Texas, home of Porter's beloved Texas A&M University.

Aggie memorabilia joined Cajun artifacts on the walls and the bar mirror. Porter's "Aggie 2" license plate let folks know where the boss's loyalty lay. At the Cadillac, the Aggies were always champs, regardless of how the annual Thanksgiving Day matchup against the tea-sippin' Longhorns turned out.

Porter's lifelong commitment to the university included an endowed presidential scholarship, a 12th Man endowed scholarship, and service as an international ambassador of goodwill and class agent for decades.

Each spring at the Border Olympics track and field meet in Laredo, Porter treated the A&M team to dinner.

Randy Matson, class of 1967, was a world champion track and field athlete. He won a silver medal in the shot put at the 1964 Olympics in Tokyo, and the gold in 1968 in Mexico City. Matson worked for the Texas A&M Association of Former Students from 1972 until 1999, when he retired after twenty years as executive director.

Randy Matson: *The Border Olympics was a big trip for us on the A&M track team. It was a long bus ride, but we always got a wonderful reception from Porter. He would have the whole track team from A&M at the Cadillac and treat us to a steak dinner. I can remember how the athletes from other schools couldn't quite understand why a former student would do that, and they were very envious of us. Of course we enjoyed rubbing it in. We just knew we were special to your dad. And what a great lesson for a bunch of young Aggies.*

One year when the team was headed south to the Border Olympics, Matson flew north to Detroit, where he was the only athlete from A&M to qualify for the NCAA Indoor Championship meet. Matson placed first in the shot put and discus.

Matson: *Porter and some other Aggies arranged for me to compete on Saturday night in Detroit and catch an early morning flight to Dallas on Sunday morning. In Dallas, they had a small private plane (I barely fit in it) waiting for me, and we flew to Laredo. If I remember right, we landed about four in the afternoon and at six I was throwing the shot in Laredo. I did miss the steak dinner, however.*

Matson recalled listening to stories he heard from the war-years Aggies about their A&M days and their army days, men such as Porter, A. W. "Head" Davis, Frank Litterst, and Dick Haas.

"What I admired most about your dad and his generation of Aggies is how much they cared about each other. They truly were a band of brothers," Matson said.

Laredo native Hector Gutierrez echoed the rewards derived from the Aggie brotherhood. Gutierrez, who became the first Hispanic commander of the Corps of Cadets in 1968, refers to himself as an Aggie *hermanito*.

As president of the Laredo A&M Club, Porter congratulated Hector Gutierrez on his selection as colonel of the A&M Corps of Cadets, 1968.

Hector Gutierrez: *When I was announced as corps commander in 1968 and I had the privilege of being the first Hispanic named to that post, Porter was one of the first to call me to express joy and gratitude. I did not know how special an honor it was until Porter pounded the significance into my naive head.*

Gutierrez, class of '69, spent his career as a public affairs consultant. He served on the boards of both the Association of Former Students and Texas A&M University Press, and was founding chairman of the Texas A&M Hispanic Network.

Gutierrez said his bond with Porter was created by Porter's friendship with his grandfather Teodosio Gutierrez. The Aggie connection added an extra dimension and enhanced their special relationship.

While Gutierrez was still at A&M, he registered for an expensive study abroad in Poland. Porter spearheaded a fundraising effort within the Laredo Aggie Club and from business leaders such as banker Max Mandel. At the airport on the day of Hector's departure, Porter gave him a check that paid for his trip.

Gutierrez: *To Porter, Aggieland represented familia, a strong, special, and firm bond. Being an Aggie was an experience of unity, love, and lifelong friendship that knew no bounds.*

That Aggie spirit prevailed at the Cadillac until my father locked the door that last night in 1979, the sign under the clock proclaiming *Texas Aggies—1967 Southwest Conference Champions.*

After Porter agreed to join Mayo at the Cadillac, he discovered that work permits in Mexico were far more difficult to acquire than in the frontier era of the twenties, when Mayo immigrated by simply filling out a form, having his picture taken, and paying twenty dollars.

Even with prominent Nuevo Laredo friends helping Porter get the *inmigrado* status, somehow the paperwork kept falling through the cracks. It took almost twelve years for the permit to be approved, finally giving Porter a temporary Mexican passport that was good for one year. At the end of that first year, he got a passport that was good for five years. After that, he was a full-fledged immigrant.

Porter: *At first I was over there working illegally and always fearful that someone would walk in and charge me with violating immigration laws. When certain officials were in town, I'd just sit at a table like a customer and tell the boys what to do. I stayed out of the kitchen and away from the bar.*

For a long time, the Mexican government looked the other way. Eventually a senator in northern Mexico arranged it so they wouldn't bother me. The Mexican customs people just assumed I had a permit. Here's the kicker. In the back of the passport, it restricted me from working in banking, freight, or bars or nightclubs. However, it also specifically stated that I came to Nuevo Laredo to manage a place known as the Cadillac Bar.

Out of necessity, Porter eventually became fluent in Spanish, easily switching between languages depending on the conversation, sometimes mixing languages in the familiar borderland lingo of Tex-Mex.

Mayo never mastered Spanish, relying on a pidgin mix of English, French, and his kitchen-Spanish vocabulary. At home he and my grandmother spoke Cajun French and followed routines transported from the bayous to the border. Mayo expected the Cadillac employees to learn English and to help them along. He spoke loudly, as though higher volume would enhance their comprehension.

My grandfather was always an early riser, waking hours before dawn to brew his chicory coffee and eat breakfast while it was still dark. Then he would drive downtown and have another coffee with his buddy Dick Meisner, who ran the Hamilton Hotel.

Every working day, until he was in his late sixties, he would be at the Cadillac by six-thirty a.m.

In later years, as Mayo slowed down and spent less time across the river, I enjoyed many childhood mornings at my grandparents' home, alternating between the kitchen, watching my maternal grandmother, whom I called Mamo, roll biscuits and set out the fig preserves. In the dark, velvet-curtained living room, I played the piano and waited for breakfast.

Mayo Bessan behind the bar, 1945.

Often I'd linger in their bedroom, watching my grandfather undertake his own morning ritual: primping in front of the full-length mirror, appraising his reflection.

Clothes made this man, and Mayo was meticulous about his appearance throughout his life, even during the leanest times in New Orleans, when starched celluloid collars were hard to come by and there was no money for new shoes or even to replace the worn soles on his black and white spectators.

I loved to watch him set the scene for his daily routine: shaving strop, straight razor, Clubman soap and aftershave lined up on his vanity counter, ready for service. I would watch as he fastened his collar and cuffs to the gold studs on his shirt, twisting the cuff links into compliance, tacked the diamond tiepin into place just between the second and third buttons, tucked a monogrammed handkerchief into his breast pocket, and aligned the front pleats of his trousers with his shoelaces.

Later in the day, after his nap, Mayo would have another shave at the Hamilton Hotel barbershop en route to his evening shift at the Cadillac.

In the New Orleans days, regardless of how hot the cards had been the night before or how late he stumbled back to his boardinghouse, Mayo's morning ablutions never wavered. Impatient for the big mirror in the bathroom at the end of the hall, Mayo would be up at four-thirty for his first coffee, dripped on the hot plate in his room, thick, dark as the night outside, and aromatic with the chicory that revived him all of his days.

So it was and always would be—coffee, bath, shave, hair combing, clothes, final inspection, and admiration.

Porter's daily discipline in the Corps of Cadets at A&M, and then in the Army, prepared him for the clock-challenging rigors of working split shifts at the Cadillac: fifteen-hour days consisting of prep work before opening, lunch, and closing. He would typically go home for a nap and to rest his legs and back before returning for the dinner service. It was a brutal schedule for a young man starting a family. Vacations were rare, since summers and holidays were the busiest times at the Cadillac.

Porter: *When I first went to work there, I'd get there about eight-thirty. The boys in the kitchen came on at nine o'clock. I'd stay until one or two o'clock in the afternoon, depending on the lunch business. Then I'd go back about four-thirty or five and stay until we closed up, ten o'clock.*

During the summers, the Cadillac was crammed with customers—eating, drinking, and escaping the pavement-melting heat. Fall and the holidays attracted large crowds as people came to Laredo to hunt and to Nuevo Laredo for Christmas shopping. The Friday after Thanksgiving was the biggest revenue day of the year.

Porter: *I knew historically how much beer to have on hand. And of course the Carta Blanca distributorship was just across the street.*

Each of the iceboxes under the bar could hold eight to ten cases of beer, depending on whether they were the big bottles or little ones. These were real iceboxes, not refrigerators. We had an ice grinder and made bar ice out of fifty-pound blocks of ice. We reloaded the boxes as they got low and when there was a lull in business. There were four more big boxes in the back.

Like clockwork, the Mexican tax auditor showed up on the Monday after Thanksgiving, ready to audit the books. The inspector would tally up the previous Friday's sales and use that amount to set taxes for the entire year, no matter that business was dead in January. It was a government-driven racket that affected most lucrative businesses in Nuevo Laredo.

Bullfight weekends always brought big crowds, bigger depending on who was in the ring. The bullfights started at four o'clock Sunday afternoon at the Plaza de Toros, so folks would have lunch at the Cadillac and linger until it was time to make the short drive to the bullring. Rafael Longoria staged the bullfights. He owned a liquor store and was an agent for Dos Equis, the Moctezuma brewery. When he died, his son, Lauro Luis Longoria, took over.

Porter: When Rafael first started staging the bullfights in the 1920s, he borrowed $500 from Mayo for his cash flow. He did that for the first two or three bullfights. And after that it was a good-luck charm, and Rafael always borrowed $100 or so from Mayo before each bullfight.

Mayo's support for bullfighting caused tension at home, drawing criticism from my grandmother Odette, an animal lover who raised chickens for eggs but never killed one for the stewpot.

Bullfight at Nuevo Laredo's Plaza de Toros, 1938.

Porter arranged his schedule around A&M football games. Enjoying pregame revelry are Genita Davis, author, Wanda Garner, Richard Cash, Porter, and Head Davis.

Porter: *One Sunday afternoon, Mayo and Odette took out-of-town friends to the bullfight. This was unusual for Odette, who hated the whole idea of bullfighting, but she went along. They were seated in the sombra, shade, near family friends Huicho Peña, Hogue Poole, and Joe Finley.*

All of a sudden a bull, enraged by the picador spears in his neck, jumped over the barrier and into the stands, headed right for the Bessans. Huicho and Joe pulled their pocketknives and stabbed the animal until it was subdued. True story. It was Odette's first and last bullfight.

In later years, with trusted managers in place, Porter arranged his time off around his main extracurricular pursuits: A&M's home football games and deer season.

Porter: *Mayo retired in 1960. When he said I was taking over, that was it. He didn't hold on. Never offered unsolicited advice. Mayo had been leasing the property from the Longorias, who had acquired it from the Benavides family. Fred Longoria handled the family prop-erty holdings and took me to negotiate with his older brother, Chito, the patriarch. Chito wanted more rent, but he let me go at Mayo's rate for two years. After that, we renegotiated every two years.*

⇒ 3 ⇐

What the Cadillac Looked Like

The first, "little" Cadillac on Guerrero Street, just three blocks south of the international bridge, was on the site where the famous Marti's gift shop would eventually rise to international prominence for its jewelry, pottery, textiles, and Mexican antiques.

Mayo's first venture was a dark watering hole with a hard-packed dirt floor and an unusable fireplace. The bar was a crude countertop in front of a couple of shelves that held liquor bottles. It was strictly a drinking establishment, with no food.

About five years later, when the Pan-American Highway construction forced him to move, Mayo found a bar for rent at the corner of Belden and Ocampo, the languishing Caballo Blanco. This former apartment building, with high cinder-block walls and

Waiters and a customer at the first Cadillac on Calle Guerrero, known in family lore as the "little Cadillac," 1929. Mayo leased this first bar location, on Guerrero, from the father of Memo Salinas-Puga. This corner site eventually became Marti Suneson's eponymous boutique and home furnishings store, Marti's.

Wanda Mae would accompany Mayo to the Cadillac on Saturday mornings, where she would play with the mostly tame animals in the parking lot menagerie. Over the years, he had monkeys, deer, parrots, cockatiels, and a tame Mexican black bear, which famously escaped and enjoyed several adventures before being corralled in the ladies room.

driveways surrounding an interior courtyard, became the "big" Cadillac that enriched and enlivened my family for more than half a century.

When Mayo took over, there were still a couple of small apartments opening onto the gravel courtyard. He converted one into a storeroom and kept the second for his own use, nights when he played poker until dawn or was too drunk or too tired to go home. Not long after Porter joined the business in 1947, Mayo gave the apartment to the night watchman, Juan Mendieta.

The courtyard parking area was also home to Mayo's menagerie, which included not-so-wild animals that hunter friends would occasionally drop off. Mayo believed the animals would be an attraction.

White-tailed deer and various species of monkey shared a corral and makeshift cages in the gravel lot, along with an anteater, a Mexican black bear, and a mountain lion. Parrots roamed free: smart, talkative macaws and Margarita, an ancient *loro* (parrot) that moved in as a mature bird and lived in the storehouse for another twenty years.

The zookeeper was longtime employee Simon "Chango" Duran, who worked as a jack-of-all-trades for Mayo at the Cadillac and at the Bessan homes in Laredo and in the Hill Country. When he wasn't tending to "*mis bebés*," Chango squeezed limes and ran the ice grinder. He made soap for the Cadillac, using grease and lye.

Chango loved the menagerie, talked to them, supplying both sides of the conversation. He regarded the animals as his children, except for the macaws, which bit him savagely at every opportunity. His special charge was the young male bear, who liked to drink beer.

Porter: *Across the street from Cadillac, the Carta Blanca distributor had a small bar with an old pool table, but I don't think there were any cue sticks or balls. One day the bear got out of his pen and started wandering around, not causing any problems. Chango goes looking for the bear and tracks it to the bar just in time to see the bear lumber in through the open front door and four or five customers tumble out through the windows. Mayo gave the saloon owner $10 for the felt he said the bear scratched off the pool table.*

When the cavernous banquet room wasn't occupied by poker players and gamblers, large parties filled the space, with serapes on the walls and straw-bottomed chairs counting as atmosphere. Due to political reforms in Mexico, Mayo and Porter didn't resume the gambling when they reopened in 1955.

Young, curious, and mostly nonthreatening, the bear was notorious for slipping away while Chango cleaned his pen. On one such occasion, my grandfather was working in his little office when he heard a ruckus down the hall.

Wanda Bessan Garner: *The voice was familiar. It was our family friend Irene Moore, yelling from the ladies' room, summoning Mayo to come get the bear that had followed her.*

The original "big" Cadillac was a sprawling space, with a main dining room and the bar and a smaller dining room. There was also a large banquet room with a small stage. It was a cavernous space built out of wood, with high windows all around the room, just under the cool gloom of the exposed beam ceiling, which was fourteen feet high. Serapes on the walls and straw-bottomed chairs counted as atmosphere.

Mayo always had a card game going in that big back room, and there were slot machines and tables for roulette and craps. Fancy drinks and French food found new fans in Nuevo Laredo, but in the early days it was gambling that made Mayo rich.

In the main dining room, assorted round and square wooden tables and chairs were positioned around thick columns. White linen tablecloths were de rigueur, as were the black bow ties and formal white jackets on the waiters and bartenders. Mayo wanted

Fourth of July at the Cadillac Bar, 1936.

In his quest to brand the Cadillac as an exclusive venue, Mayo ordered fancy china from Loubat in New Orleans. For special family occasions, I use the few remaining pieces in my personal collection.

to offer the same dining refinement he admired in New Orleans, down to the Cadillac embroidery copying the same red script used by Galatoire's in New Orleans.

The carved mahogany bar had a brass footrail and well-used spittoons. An ornately carved back bar had a marble-topped counter, beveled mirrors, and liquor bottles artfully arranged.

Light fixtures and ceiling fans with pull strings dotted the

In this 1955 photo, the author takes up her favorite position at the Cadillac: astride Pancho Villa's saddle, on Easter 1954, three months before the flood.

pressed-tin ceiling. Central air conditioning and heat weren't installed until the renovations after the 1954 flood.

The walls were crowded with photographs of New Orleans and south Louisiana, alongside pictures of hunting trophies, quail, deer, and stringers of fat fish.

And of course there was always the prime conversation starter: Pancho Villa's saddle. Generations of children climbed onto the wrought-iron stand that held the saddle and grinned as parents took their pictures.

The dark leather was embossed and tooled with an intricate Aztec design, from the side jockey pieces down to the fenders and stirrups. Sterling silver sheathed the pommel, the conchas, and the stirrup treads.

Mounted on the wall behind the saddle was a framed photograph of Pancho Villa on a white horse, astride the saddle.

Porter: *Once when Mayo was in Mexico City to call on O. A. Carles, who had a distillery and made gin for the Cadillac, Carles showed*

Wanda Bessan Garner and her faithful canine companion Whoopie on Pancho Villa's saddle, 2002.

him a saddle that had belonged to Pancho Villa. Carles told Mayo it would be a good attraction at the Cadillac, so Mayo bought it. He paid 800 pesos for the saddle, a fortune in 1932.

The saddle now sits in the library of my home in the Hill Country. Mayo's photo of Villa was lost in the flood.

The flood swept away almost everything: tables, chairs, supplies. The bar and back bar were pushed off their footings and smashed into an exterior wall, impaled by a huge tree. The stinking signature of the flood was smeared on everything in the main dining room.

After the flood, when it appeared the losses were so extensive that restoration would be prohibitively expensive, Mayo wavered about reopening. But the family council prevailed, and nine months later, the Cadillac was reborn, with a modern look layered atop that French Quarter gentility.

The banquet room, already gutted by the floodwater, was razed to make room for additional parking and a side entrance and small gift shop area. Glass cases displayed treasures from Aladar Deutsch's shop: French perfumes in artistic bottles, jewelry, and sterling cuff links.

Pancho Villa's saddle, 2019.

Terrazzo replaced the pitted concrete floors. Walls were stuccoed and painted bright white, and the windows were glazed with thick, opaque glass.

Wanda and Odette had their own decorating ideas; soon a planter bloomed with tropical specimens just inside the main

The front door, a couple of days after floodwaters reached
ten feet high inside the Cadillac.

entrance, and drapes flanked the windows. New wrought-iron
chairs with padded backrests and seats made dining more comfortable.

My UT journalism school classmate Joe Phillips tells a story of
his mother buying reclaimed chairs from the old Cadillac.

Joe Phillips: *News of the sale of the Spanish-style furniture from the
Cadillac Bar spread up and down the river. Jean Phillips, mother of
five and the wife of the McAllen Texaco consignee, decided eight
chairs would make the perfect complement for a Honduran mahogany dining table she was having made at a local cabinet shop. She
told my father, Fred Phillips Jr., of her plans to go to Laredo to buy
the chairs. He told her he wanted her to buy locally, but she ignored
him, grabbed a friend, and the two ladies embarked for Laredo in
the Phillips family's station wagon. Those eight chairs graced the
family dining room for the next fifty years and are now in the home
of one of her sons, along with the mahogany table.*

On a shopping trip to New Orleans, Odette and Wanda bought
antique mirrors and marble-topped consoles from Abe Manheim's
store on Royal Street. They found sepia-tone photographs of the
bayou country and had them framed for the dining room.

Interior of the Cadillac Bar, 1970.

Mayo and Porter flanked by Ruben Chacon and Porfirio Robles on the day the Cadillac reopened on April 1, 1955, after being closed for nine months following the 1954 flood.

Businessmen on both sides of the river favored the Cadillac for power lunches. In the foreground table are Tad Brittingham and Fernando Zuniga. Longtime waiter Francisco Segovia faces the camera at the left.

The ladies' restroom was remodeled, with French mirrors, wallpaper, and marble-topped vanities. The men's restroom, though restored to its previous utilitarian function, never approached the same level of comfort or decor.

Modern climate control saw the old ceiling fans and gas space heaters give way to central air conditioning, perhaps the single best remodeling investment, considering Laredo's summer temperatures ranged from an average of 98 in May to 100 in August.

Summers were brutal, and the streets in Nuevo Laredo were empty, even of tourists, from noon until four. When sweaty shoppers entered the swinging front doors of the Cadillac after a hot sidewalk trek from the mercado or Marti's, the new air conditioning swaddled them in a blast of icy air.

The Cadillac's refinements of linen tablecloths and napkins and waiter uniforms inspired other fine dining spots in Nuevo Laredo, as Mexican entrepreneurs copied Mayo's style, if not his substance.

The Cadillac was never a fancy place, but on the Texas-Mexico border, it was the place to be.

The Cast of Characters

The Cadillac attracted a number of colorful characters, home-grown and from far away. They came for the drinks and stayed for the food.

"Where Old Friends Meet" was the Cadillac's advertising slogan for years, on bumper stickers, T-shirts, and matchbooks. The faithful customers were unique to Laredo, a microcosm hard to explain to outsiders who wouldn't understand the eccentric behavior and conspicuous consumption displayed by the iconoclastic residents of the border town.

"Something in the water," observers would mumble.

The people and the geography gave Laredo its *enweirdments*. Exhibiting a fierce independence older than the United States and a pioneer determination blended with European and Latin American sensibilities, "los dos Laredos" bridged cultures and class to create a community of hardworking, hard-living individualists.

Russell Deutsch, who for more than forty years ran the family business founded by his father Aladar Deutsch in 1929, believes the success of Deutsch's jewelry store and the Cadillac was rooted in border-town geography.

Russell Deutsch: *None of our businesses would ever have succeeded so well if they had been anywhere else. It was Nuevo Laredo that defined us, a combination of everything—the bullfights, Boy's Town, Marti's, Deutsch's, and the Cadillac. Where we were made all the difference in the world.*

In the thirties and forties, Aladar Deutsch and Mayo Bessan, recognizing that geographical opportunity, were early entrepreneurs on

A bevy of young Laredo women outside Deutsch's, including Lola De Llano Jackson, Gloria Longoria Padilla, Blanca De Llano Cooper, and Mary Rose De Llano Smith. Photo courtesy of Glen Jackson..

the Mexican side of the river, laying the foundations for landmarks that would become beacons of the vibrant tourism that created fortunes on both sides of the border.

Aladar Deutsch emigrated from Hungary to Mexico because quotas kept him out of the United States. He married Eva Torchin of Laredo, and they opened a small curio shop on Calle Guerrero, Nuevo Laredo's main street. Later the store expanded to include imported perfumes and then the custom jewelry that became Deutsch's famed hallmark. Mrs. Deutsch was the elegant doyenne who presided regally over the shop, cosseting favorite customers as they harvested baubles and elegant bottles of French cologne.

Jean Claire Garner Turcotte, Porter's sister and lifelong friends with Russell Deutsch, has drawers filled with jewelry from Deutsch's. She cherishes a silver jewelry case from Deutsch's that Mayo's best friend, Al Roschuni, gave her as a high school graduation present.

My sister Clay and I had our ears pierced at Deutsch's, spirited there by Suzy Mayo one Sunday afternoon without our mother's knowledge. Amparo Flores, a glamorous and intimidating saleswoman who wore a fortune in gems on every finger, in her earlobes, and around her neck, used an ancient and pain-free piercing method. First, she would swab the lobes with alcohol, press them between two pieces of ice, and then stab through the flesh with a needle. It really didn't hurt, didn't bleed, and didn't get infected. The piercing was free, unless you count the bill Mr. Deutsch sent my father for two pairs of pearl and diamond earrings.

Neighboring business owners in Nuevo Laredo became close friends, from Mayo to Porter to people in my generation. Family friendships with the Longorias, Franks, Sunesons, and Deutsches endure to this day.

Just down the block from the Cadillac was the Acapulco gift shop, owned by Mauricio Frank. He married Adela Bautista, who emigrated with her family from Istanbul, Turkey, to Mexico and

Mayo used "nuf sed," one of his trademark sayings, in this economic development brochure promoting Laredo. That was misspelled purposely, in contrast to the typographical error on "quisine."

eventually Nuevo Laredo. Adela's sister, Marti, worked in the shop before founding her own eponymous boutique, filled with glorious indigenous textiles, artifacts, and antiques.

Marti's son Jack Suneson grew the business, building an architecturally spectacular new store with a landscaped courtyard and two floors of handmade clothing embroidered and embellished by Mexican seamstresses, furniture and ceramics, and luxurious accessories.

Because we were children of business owners in Mexico, Jack and I and Jack's cousin, Jaque Frank, claimed the main streets and backstreets of Nuevo Laredo as our private playground, afoot or in one of Jack's cool cars, stopping in at our parents' businesses for money to buy coco con chile (coconut with chili powder) and elotes (grilled Mexican corn on the cob) from the street vendors.

In 1975, I bought my wedding dress at Marti's, as Jack and Richard, my husband-to-be, nodded their approval. The day before my wedding, Jack showed up at my parents' house with a set of hand-painted Mexican china I had admired.

Jack became close to my father and ate lunch at the Cadillac every day for years, swapping stories about government corruption and painful *mordidas* (slang for bribes) and scheming how to increase tourism to Nuevo Laredo. Theirs was an unexpected friendship. Even in the late sixties and seventies, when my father would turn away young men whose hair was too long or girls whose skirts were too short, Porter always welcomed Jack, shaggy-haired and bearded, wearing sandals and patchouli oil.

Jack Suneson: *The Cadillac Bar and Porter Garner were synonymous with Nuevo Laredo. Porter treated everyone as an equal. Whether [he was dealing with] the parking attendant or the CEO of a big company, he was a gentleman who knew how to treat people.*

Facing lost business from increasing turmoil and violence from the Mexican drug wars on the border, Jack closed the Nuevo Laredo store and opened in a new location in San Antonio in 2009. He died in 2015.

Russell Deutsch endured similar stresses at the jewelry store.

Hordes of shoppers who once filled Nuevo Laredo, disembarking from chartered buses and private planes, dwindled to a few hearty souls who ventured across an almost-deserted bridge.

The drug violence in Mexico in the mid-2000s hurt border businesses in two ways. Tourists stopped coming to Nuevo Laredo, while Mexicans started leaving their country in what was dubbed the "Mexodus" by the Borderzine student journalism project documenting the flight of middle-class families to the United States.

Russell Deutsch: *I don't think anybody ever visualized the extent of cartel dominance. We didn't expect it would get so bad. Everybody was telling me it was time to get out, so I decided to retire.*

Deutsch, who reopened his jewelry store in Laredo after shuttering the original Mexican location in 2003, said leaving Nuevo Laredo was one of the hardest decisions of his life. "I loved Nuevo Laredo and Mexico and everything about it. It was a way of life and all I knew," he said.

Deutsch and Porter had shared a similar trajectory in Nuevo Laredo, becoming part of a family business neither had previously considered an option, suffering through the immigration process at about the same time, hiding from government inspectors always ready to extract a mordida from the till.

They also shared an accountant and a flamboyant friend, a Mrs. Camacho, owner of Papagallos, the biggest and most popular brothel in Boy's Town, Nuevo Laredo's red-light district. Over many lunches, the unlikely trio would lament the petty corruption and consider how to avoid paying bribes.

Russell Deutsch: *Porter and I had a unique friendship, ultimate trust. We never really socialized, but we were friends and partners on many business ventures. We did a lot of deals and never made much money.*

The Longoria family figured prominently in the Cadillac's history and its success, beginning in 1924, with Don Octaviano and his wife Sara befriending Mayo and his young bride.

Epitacio Resendez, A&M Class of 1988, on Pancho Villa's saddle. Photo courtesy of Epitacio Resendez.

The Longoria children, grandchildren, and extended family were our friends, our landlords, and ultimately the owners of the Cadillac Bar. Don Octaviano's eldest son, Chito, controlled the property where the Cadillac stood at the intersection of Ocampo and Belden. His brother Fred negotiated the lease. When Porter closed the Cadillac in 1979, monthly rent was $2,000.

Another Nuevo Laredo character was my father's dear friend, Epitacio Resendez, who used the Cadillac's phone number on his business card. Resendez was from a prominent Nuevo Laredo ranching family and a proud Aggie. Although he was officially Texas A&M Class of '48, he actually finished his degree in 1946 at the age of seventeen.

His son Epitacio, class of '99, divides his time between San Antonio and Budapest, Hungary.

Epitacio R. Resendez: *My memories of the Cadillac Bar are many, since my family's life revolves around it and your father. If money needed to be put away, it was at your dad's huge safe. If it was beer to be purchased before going to the ranch at five a.m., it was there.*

If we wanted dinner to take out, it was there. My dad would visit the
Cadillac two or three times a day. He would stand next to the phone
at the end of the bar and answer the phone, because most of the
calls were for him anyway.

At the other end of the bar, Porter's other compadre, Chuck
Jacaman, staked out his spot, close to the kitchen doors. Chuck,
a Laredo legend known for his entrepreneurism and love of fast
motorcycles, was a daily customer at the Cadillac. His family immigrated to Mexico from Palestine and eventually settled on the
American side of the river.

Chuck would stop at the mercado each morning to buy
fresh panela cheese. He and my father would make it their second breakfast, sharing a plate and squeezing lime juice over the
stringy pieces they pulled from the ball of mozzarella-like cheese.
Hot bolillos slathered with butter and sometimes a dish of refried
beans rounded out their midmorning treat.

Chuck and his family lived in Montrose, around the corner from
our house on Malinche. His eldest daughter, Linda, has been my best

The Jacaman family celebrated daughter Linda's high school graduation at the Cadillac in 1967. Pictured, left to right: Denise, Fairris, Chuck
holding Tracy, Bobby, Linda, and Chuck Jr. Photo courtesy of Fairris
Jacaman.

friend for more than fifty years. She married Buddy Bruni, whose mother was Lilia Longoria, one of Don Octaviano's daughters.

During the Cadillac's second heyday, from the late 1950s to its closing, Suzy Mayo easily was the best-informed, best-connected woman in Laredo. Suzy was popular, pretty, and handy with a story, and her wit and spicy tongue drew people to her regular table at the Cadillac, much as Porter's quiet amiability drew customers through the front door.

Her recollections of the luncheons, parties, and dinners paint a half-century panorama of revelers and drunks, escapades and enduring friendships.

Suzy Mayo: *I was a war bride, thought it would be so romantic, going from one post to another. We never left Laredo, but we had going-away dinners for three years, just thinking Jim would be shipped out any day.*

Jim said his very first outing after he got to Laredo was to the Cadillac Bar. He walked up to the only big round table in the place. Seated around the table, men contemplated stacks of money in front of them. Jim said one man was wearing gray suede gloves. That was old man [Henry] Jackson. A waiter told Jim the men were Mr. Bessan's card buddies and they were settling up their annual accounts.

During the war, we had to save stamps to buy a steak or bacon. People would go across the river to eat at the Cadillac and stop at the butcher shop on the way home. Eventually the Mexicans put their foot down and prohibited exporting bacon, so people would smuggle it across. In the summertime, the bacon fat would melt in pools on their floorboard.

Suzy and my mother were best friends, growing up together, raising children together, and spending long lunches and dinners together at the Cadillac.

Suzy: *We went to Wanda and Porter's wedding. Mother and Dad went, too. She always told Wanda she'd never forget her wedding day because it was the day her cow Esperanza died.*

One night Wanda and I were sitting at the Cadillac. All of a sudden those swinging doors opened up and this character backed in all the way to the bar, like someone was chasing him, looking around the room frantically. It was like out of a movie. The man kept his back to the bar and his eyes on the swinging door, ordering shots one after another. Porter told us later that his name was El Gato and that he was a regular, but that he never talked.

Turns out that El Gato was an airman stationed at the Laredo Air Force Base. When he came in through the swinging front doors, he'd step off to one side, like he didn't want to leave himself in the open. He always stood at the end of the bar by the telephone, and he always kept his right hand free. After a while he'd make a sudden movement, as if he was drawing a pistol, pretend to shoot at something behind the bar, and go "Pow!"

One night Ramón Salido, who claimed a regular table in the corner by the planter, beat El Gato to the draw. Salido walked up to him and said, "You're pretty good with that six-gun. What's your handle?"

The fellow grinned and blew on his right index finger. "South of the Rye-o-Grande they call me El Gato. North of here they call me the Cat."

Ramón said, "I'm pretty good, too," and proceeded to draw his own "gun" and "shoot" at an imaginary target behind the bar. The competition went back and forth for a while. Then Ramón said, "You missed!"

El Gato, still grinning, said, "I never shoulda gambled south of the Rye-o-Grande."

Bill Mayo: *My grandparents Cricket and George Neel were regulars at the Cadillac, with their best friends Hazel and Dick Powell. Cricket and Hazel also loved going to lunch across the river with Marjorie Zachry, who was Dick Powell's sister.*

Once Cricket called Porter to warn him to "watch those bartenders" because they were putting "mickeys" into her drinks. Cricket's standard order was a double old-fashioned. One Palm Sunday, after church and lunch at the Cadillac, she told us she went right home

Suzy Mayo's mother was Bess "Cricket" Neel, who hosted
a luncheon in November 1946, for a visitor named Nellie.
Cricket is on the far left, while Suzy is on the far right.
Others familiar faces were Rose Houser, Diana Lafon, Odette
Martin, Hazel Powell, and Marjorie Zachry. Photo courtesy
of Bill Mayo.

and went to bed with her shoes on. She said she had only two old-
fashioneds and that they were "mild."

I also remember the time Emma Leigh Zachry took a Zachry
company plane and flew to Laredo with Peter Ustinov and Jonathan
Winters and spent the day at the Cadillac.

Odette and Mayo lived on Aldama Street in the Montrose neighborhood in southeast Laredo, and their good friends Emma and Henry Zachry lived in a big house around the corner. Their son, H.B., known as Pat, graduated from A&M and went to work as a surveyor in Laredo, where his father owned the Merchants State Bank.

Pat Zachry married Dick Powell's sister Marjorie, and they had five children: Mary Pat, who married Louis Stumberg (Patio Ranch in Hunt); Bartell; Jimmy; Suzanne, who married Tim Word; and Emma Leigh, who married David Carter.

The Montrose neighborhood, east of downtown, was one of Laredo's first suburbs, with imposing brick and stucco homes that sprawled over entire blocks, next to modest bungalows and empty fields where cows grazed on the cliffs above Chacon Creek.

Porter: *Eventually my parents moved to Montrose and also lived on Aldama, a couple blocks down from the Bessans. After Wanda and I married, we lived in one of Fred Werner's rent houses on Malinche Street, until we built our own house farther down the street with cinder blocks we made ourselves.*

Mayo and Odette were friendly with the Zachrys and with Harvey and Louise Mecom, parents of wildcatter John Mecom Sr., who developed the oil fields in Saudi Arabia. The Mecoms lived on the Bar Nothing Ranch near San Ygnacio, where Harvey and Mayo spent idle afternoons fishing for bass in his vast stock tanks.

Porter: *Old man Mecom and Mayo were good friends, and Harvey and Louise loved to eat at the Cadillac. Mrs. Mecom was a grand old lady. She loved mangoes, and we'd keep them on ice for her. She'd stop in and pick up the mangoes and have her driver take her to a park by the river and she'd sit on a bench and eat her mangoes.*

The Mecoms bought quite a few things for the ranch from Edgar Mims at the Border Foundry tool and machine shop in Laredo. Mrs. Mecom went in there one day, and someone was playing with a pair of dice on the counter. Edgar said after a while everybody, including Mrs. Mecom, was down on the floor shooting dice for 50-cent stakes.

Opening day of white-winged dove season. Fall was a favorite time for visiting Webb County. Pictured here are Cadillac regulars Annette and Bob Ross of Corpus Christi. Photo from the collection of Chula Ross Sanchez.

Years later, John Mecom built a Spanish-style hacienda at his own ranch north of San Ygnacio, where he filled the pastures with exotic animals and the house with celebrity visitors, including the shah of Iran. He had his airstrip extended to accommodate the shah's plane. State troopers shut down Highway 83 whenever the plane landed because it had to fly in low over the highway.

Porter: *Once John brought Willie Shoemaker to the Cadillac for lunch. A regular customer, a fellow nicknamed Sapo, couldn't get over how small Shoemaker was and finally just picked the jockey* *up under the arms like you would a child. Shoemaker was good-natured about the ribbing.*

Just as sure as Texas hunters circled their calendars for the start of dove season and white-tailed deer, generations of their wives and daughters used to mark the fall with road trips to Nuevo Laredo for Christmas shopping at Marti's and Deutsch's, punctuated by lazy lunches at the Cadillac.

Lynn Pugh Remadna: *A group of us gals from Austin would charter a bus and go down to Laredo each fall to shop. We started at the Cadillac, then went through the market and then to a little bar on the back side of the market, then back through the market and other shops, and then back to the Cadillac. The best was a few Ramos gin fizzes and frog legs with fries and a shrimp cocktail. Yum. Wish it was still there and times were better.*

One of those frequent early visitors was Elizabeth Harte Owens, who grew up in Corpus Christi, a daughter of legendary Texas newspaperman Ed Harte. Owens, known as Biddy, has lived in Boston since 1972 and calls herself a "homesick Texan."

Among her favorite memories of the Cadillac were visits marshaled by the Hartes' family friend Annette Ross and Ross's daughters.

Biddy Harte Owens: *I remember in the late fifties or early sixties, walking in with Big Annette and her entourage on a Saturday night during a hunting weekend and having everybody in the place come over and visit with her. On our day trips, after parking the car, we'd walk to the market and buy mangoes and give them to our waiter to chill. After lunch, he would present them, peeled and resting on a plate of shaved ice.*

In the late sixties, my boyfriend Tim Connolly and I would drive to Nuevo Laredo just for the night on a date. I told my parents we were going to Padre Island for a party. Once we parked in the Cadillac lot and went out on the town. Hours later, when we came back to get the car, the battery was dead. I decided I could not stay there overnight and risk the wrath of my parents, so I took a taxi from Laredo to Corpus Christi, asking the driver to let me out one street over so they wouldn't hear me arrive.

Will Harte, Biddy Harte's brother, remembers going to the Cadillac as a ten-year-old, after the family moved to Corpus Christi from San Angelo. He said his "Yankee mother," New Hampshire–born Janet Frey, caught on quickly about the best spots in South Texas, guided by their next-door neighbor, Annette Ross, who introduced the Harte family to the pleasures of the Cadillac.

Biddy became fast friends with Annette's daughters, Chula Ross Sanchez and Gayle Ross DeGeurin, who shared their own recollections of the Cadillac and their mother Big Annette and her friends in Laredo.

Gayle Ross DeGeurin: *It was for a good reason my mama, Annette, wanted a bit of her ashes spread in the Cadillac Bar's parking lot. We thought of it as a home away from home. Carefree days of*

Will Harte spearheaded two refurbishments of the Cadillac Bar sign, including a second repair by Tim Ross of the Neon Gallery in Houston after most of the neon tubing broke during a trip to Kerrville to show the sign to Porter. Photo courtesy of Will Harte.

roaming the market and back for a cold Coca-Cola or lemonade, yummy bolillos, tostadas y frijoles.

Later during our escapades with high school and college buddies, Chula and I did not realize that Porter and half of Texas would report to our mother and grandparents about how nice it was to see us. Yikes! Caught!

Gayle's husband, Houston attorney Mike DeGeurin, said he had heard all the Cadillac stories from his wife and her family and friends for years.

Mike DeGeurin: *I presumed they were true. Wanting their approval kept me from misbehaving there. It always upset me when any guest disrespected the wonderful waiters. Even during our less mature, roaring drunk days, misbehaving at the Cadillac was considered disrespectful and not cool. Being overserved was something that was accepted as "happening from time to time," and how one handled himself in that condition was observed as a true reflection of character. Like closing one eye to keep a proper balance and respectful posture while navigating between tables. The Cadillac put up with very little bad behavior.*

Porter was discreet about placing people at tables so as to avoid perceived potential problems.

Gayle and Mike's son, Michael, has his own memories of going to the Cadillac with his parents. "I went to the Cadillac at least once a year from ages one until thirty years old. I miss the panchos, the bolillos with pico, margaritas to go, and most importantly, the Ramos gin fizz," he said.

Will Harte's memories include a redemption story about the Cadillac bar sign that was "rescued" from its corner outpost after Porter left Nuevo Laredo. The sign languished for many years, paint flaking and neon tubing broken.

Will Harte: *I crossed paths with the famous Cadillac bar sign and decided it needed some work. I took it to a neon place in San Antonio, where it was put back together. Then I joined a group led by* *your brother to show your dad the sign. Craig Jackson brought the sign up to Kerrville in an enclosed trailer, having laid it on a mattress to smooth out any bumps. We didn't realize that rule number one is "Don't lay a neon sign on its back." When we pulled the sign out, virtually all the tubes were broken. That didn't stop us from trying to light it up. Craig was parked in a bank parking lot. He had an extension cord and found a plug in the wall of the building among the shrubbery. The sign sparked and sputtered, and your father said, "That's about how it looked in Nuevo Laredo." Needless to say, a group of about fifteen people milling around in a bank parking lot with a neon sign that is trying to catch on fire caused someone to alert the authorities. The police pulled up and informed us that we really needed to unplug the sign and move along. We did.*

Eventually Harte had the sign repaired in Houston by Chula Sanchez's brother Tim Ross, who owns the Neon Gallery in Houston.

Matt Sjoberg belonged to one of the Austin families who throughout the 1960s and '70s made frequent weekend trips to Laredo to stay at La Posada and camp out during the day and well into the night at a large table at the Cadillac.

Helen Storey and her longtime sweetheart, Hogue Poole (waving), join the La Salle County delegation that included Kassie and John Adami. Photo courtesy of Lee Keithley Adami.

Matt Sjoberg: *We would caravan down in big Buick station wagons, the sixties precursors to the Suburban, and hopefully arrive early enough to get parking places under the cane in the shade behind the bar.*

Once in the bar, my father, Walter Sjoberg, would find Porter, usually standing next to Pancho Villa's saddle (along with the hand-written sign explaining that it had been in a flood for several days), and let him know we had twenty or so in need of a table. We always had our table before the adults drained their first drinks, and my brother and I, our Cokes.

The adults would then leave the kids in the care of the wait-ers, one named Mario in particular, while they shopped at Marti's, Deutsch's, and in the market. This was their routine practice until I was about eight and my brother six, at which time we were set free to roam around Nuevo Laredo on our own.

I vividly recall Mr. Garner directing the seating of guests; the iron furniture, the great food, and the large photographs of Mexican scenes on the walls. I also recall how much I appreciated the cold blast of the air conditioning when the swinging doors closed behind me after a foray into the heat!

My dad struck up a friendship with José Martínez, a fabulous saddle maker and leather craftsman, who had his shop on Ocampo, right across from the Cadillac. Señor Martínez was a PANista [a member of the National Action Party, the Partido Acción Nacio-nal], *and one day told Dad he had enough of the PRI* [the Institu-tional Revolutionary Party, the Partido Revolucionario Institucio-nal] *and wanted to move to the United States. Dad and former US congressman Joe Kilgore helped him do so. Señor Martínez spent some time in Cotulla, and I understand eventually landed in Ingram, where he died. As I write this message, my coffee sits on a round leather coaster bearing his stamp.*

In 2009, Dad went to La Posada, when he was eighty-four. He didn't go across. I think he just wanted to get close to his old haunts. I had the same feeling as I sat on the balcony of my river-view room at the La Posada night before last. We'd both like one more Ramos gin fizz.

Folks from "up north"—Cotulla and Freer—also crossed the Rio Grande regularly for frog legs and whiskey sours.

Three generations of Cotulla's Light family were friends and regulars at the Cadillac. The patriarch, George, was from Pilot Point, Texas. His son George Jr. married Joe Finley's cousin Billie Rae Bilbo. They had three children: George IV "Cuatro," Gary, and daughter Sarah Kathryn, who married world champion cowboy Phil Lyne.

Sidney James and his wife Kate Jordan had the mercantile in Cotulla after World War II, with a drugstore and a post office. Their store sold beer and general merchandise. After Sidney died, she married an automobile dealer in Dallas.

Other Cotulla ranchers were Jack and Ruth Maltsberger, whose son Jack married Sarah Lee Storey. Sarah's aunt Helen Storey had a prominent corner table at the Cadillac. Helen, a grande dame of Cotulla ranching royalty, was the longtime sweetheart of another ranching legend: Hogue Poole, who was part of the trio who helped save my grandmother's life at a bullfight.

Helen and Hogue never married, but they built a house together and sent out Christmas cards together. They often dined with Danny Kinsel and his wife, Dorothy Mangum. Her father was land baron Clinton Mangum, who owned most of the land from Carrizo Springs to Freer.

Porter: *General John Hodges and his wife, Claude, retired to Encinal because her father, Atlee Coleman, owned land that's now part of the Callaghan Ranch. Claude and Mary Reynolds, a retired army nurse, were longtime friends who met in the Philippines. They would come to the Cadillac at least twice a week to have lunch during shopping and errands in Laredo. Claude always ordered double martinis, very dry. I'd greet them and we'd be talking, and Claude would interrupt to say, "Before I forget it, I'll have a double martini." As the gin took hold, she and Mary would have loud arguments. Once Claude turned around and said to an adjacent table: "Don't be apprehensive, Mary and I have an agreement—all invitations and insults must be confirmed the next morning or they do not count."*

There was a bunch of San Antonio gals who would stay at La

Posada, eat at the Cadillac, and then go back and play bridge at the Posada. Katie Wood, wife of the assassinated federal judge John Wood, was among the regulars. She and I were brought into this world by the same doctor in Nixon, Texas.

Charlie Becker and his first wife, Peggy, were part of the San Antonio bunch. They were good friends and regular customers. Peggy was always the life of the party. One year, Peggy and Charlie had been to Mardi Gras, where Charlie marched in one of the parades with the San Antonio Cavaliers. After that trip, one of the San Antonio papers wrote up an item, asking what San Antonio society matron was seen dancing on a table at Pat O'Brien's in New Orleans? It was Peggy and everybody knew, even though her name wasn't used. Peggy was mad as hell that they used the term matron. *Not long after that, Peggy and her friends were at the Cadillac for*

Ernest Bruni, unwavering friend to Mayo and Porter, was both solo customer and host to lively groups. L-R: Truman Phelps, James Penn, Lilia Longoria, Bruni, Matias De Llano, Ernest Bruni, unidentified couple, and Julie Bell Phelps. Photo courtesy of Linda and Buddy Bruni.

dinner. They were leaving just as I closed for the night. The front door was locked, and they were going out the back with me.

I told Peggy she had hurt my feelings because she danced on the table in New Orleans and never at my bar. Next thing I knew, she had hoisted herself up and was strutting down the bar. I was scared to death she would fall and hurt herself, so I got her down, and they left.

Peggy didn't know my connection with Bill Hall at the South Texas Citizen. *I told Bill what to write in his "Around the Town" column and then sent a copy of the paper to all of her friends in San Antonio: "what well-known SA society matron etc."*

Sometimes it was hard for Bill Hall to convince his wife, Alice, to go home. She'd want to stay and visit. Alice loved to talk. I'd do everything to convince her, blow the fan on her, and finally Bill would just pick her up and carry her to the car, and she'd be still talking. Once there was a potato shortage in Laredo, and I gave Alice a few in a bag to take home one night. When they got to the bridge, she told customs "I have a few taters." The customs man corrected her verb tense and said she "had" them and confiscated them.

Porter: *Ed Corrigan was another Cadillac stalwart. He had a forwarding agency and had to check with Mexican customs every morning. He would have coffee and pan dulce in Laredo at the Kress basement lunch counter early. Then he'd arrive at the Cadillac through the back door before we were open, about 7:15 in the morning, for a toddy. He'd check in with customs, then come back for another toddy and a full breakfast.*

Mr. Corrigan was a fine gentleman, and a character. He would stand at the bar and answer the phone "Comandancia de policía" or "Eastside Livery Stable." That's one of the times I saw Mr. Bessan get pretty hot. Mr. Corrigan had been in pretty early when Mayo was trying to start the day. Mr. Corrigan was answering the phone and being smart-alecky.

Mr. Bessan, always polite, said, "Mr. Corrigan you've been running things for the last thirty minutes, and I'd like to tell you from now on I'm taking over."

The Brunis were prominent early Laredo settlers with an Italian background. A. M. Bruni, the patriarch, was born in Emilia-Romagna, Italy, and moved to Texas as a child to live with an uncle after his parents died. He amassed vast real estate holdings, owning more than 200,000 acres of land in South Texas when he died in 1931.

One branch of the Bruni family included siblings Ernest, Alice, and Fred. Ernest married Lilia Longoria, a sister of Chito Longoria.

Ernest and Mayo were fast friends who shared a love of telling stories, drinking bourbon, and playing poker. Long after the backroom card games ended, my father inherited Mr. Bruni's friendship. Ernest was at the Cadillac almost every day, until one day, during my father's regime, he crossed a line and told an Aggie joke that Porter Garner Jr., class of '45, found inappropriate. My father's spirited sense of humor did not extend to making fun of anything having to do with Texas A&M.

Family friend Con Mims Jr. lingers at the front door, where a sidewalk sign advertises the day's specials. Photo courtesy of Steve Mims.

When Ernest persisted in goading my father, Dad picked up Mr. Bruni's glass from the bar and asked him to leave and not come back.

The banished Bruni took his bruised feelings elsewhere for a few days. One morning about a week later, a hat sailed in through the open front door. Ernest peered around the doorframe and asked if Porter would commute his sentence. All was forgiven, and the whiskey flowed freely once more. From then on, Mr. Bruni's tall tales avoided any reference to Aggies or A&M.

The Mirando City oil boom brought lots of new people and new money to Laredo and Webb County.

Legendary wildcatter O. W. Killam's head man was "Big" Frank Staggs, whose son Frank Jr. married Julieta Farias, who died in 2015 after a long siege with Alzheimer's. Frank and Julie were childhood friends of Wanda's.

Bud Evans was in the drilling business. He and his wife, Irene, had two children, Lucy and Sam. Later, these old friends would reappear in Porter's life, as the widowed Lucy Evans Fowler moved into the Riverhill Country Club neighborhood in Kerrville and resumed a friendship with Porter's second wife, Betty Joe, who had been her maid of honor decades previous.

J. W. Edgar was the superintendent of schools in Mirando City until Porter Sr. hired him away to be his assistant superintendent in Victoria. Later, Edgar ran the schools in Orange, Texas, under Lutcher Stark and eventually became a commissioner of the Texas Education Agency.

Other Mirando City regulars at the Cadillac were Gus and Irene Becker. One of Irene's sisters, Louise, married Dr. E. M. Longoria of Laredo. Irene and Louise were daughters of "Papa" Joe Leyendecker.

Billy Gibbons, lead singer of ZZ Top, is a longtime fan of the Cadillac Bar, with an extensive collection of Cadillac memorabilia. 1976.

Billy Gibbons autographed a Cadillac Bar napkin for the author, 2017.

The Mims brothers, Con and Ed, profited from the boom as their Border Foundry hardware and welding service supplied the oil fields. Ed lived in Mirando City and ran the operation there, while Con lived in Laredo and ran the business on Market Street.

Con married Mary Margaret "Mammy" Irwin, and they had three sons: Con Jr., who was killed in World War II; Bill; and Edgar, who carried on the family business. Today Con's grandson "Pancho" Mims runs the Weston Tools operation in Monterrey.

Celebrities were abundant at the Cadillac, and Porter was always the affable host.

Among the notable regulars were Pedro Armendáriz Sr.; Leo Carrillo, the Cisco Kid's sidekick; Katy Jurado; and Mario Moreno, better known as Cantinflas.

"Big Kyle" Ervin would bring folks who were in town to go quail hunting. Dizzy Dean and Phil Harris came every fall. Once Ervin brought Roy Rogers and Jack Dempsey in for dinner. Big Kyle introduced the cowboy crooner to Porter, noting that Rogers didn't drink.

When Rogers asked for a sarsaparilla, Porter obliged. He always had a few bottles of the sweet soda pop stashed away, along with other exotic choices, ever ready for the odd request.

In the late forties, cowboy actor Sunset Carson hung out at the bar, on off days while his movie company was filming *Rio Grande* in Laredo. Cadillac regulars Bobby Deats and Crispin Martin were in the movie, and regaled customers with tales from the dusty set and raves about the actress who played the movie's heroine, Evohn Keyes.

Andy Gault, who was born in Laredo and grew up down the street in our Montrose neighborhood, now lives in California. He recalls a personal connection to movie stars who stayed in Laredo while filming *Viva Zapata!* in nearby San Ygnacio in 1951. Not only did Marlon Brando and Anthony Quinn show up at the Cadillac for dinner several times, they liked the local baseball team.

Andy Gault: *My uncle Fred Leyendecker played for the Laredo Apaches for many seasons. In 1950 or '51 we were at a game watching him play, and Marlon Brando, Anthony Quinn, and other movie stars were in the stands watching the game.*

In later years, another notable fan was guitarist Billy Gibbons of ZZ Top, who amassed a collection of Cadillac memorabilia.

⇒ 5 ⇐

The Flood

Wednesday, June 30, 1954, sunrise.

The weather report on San Antonio's WOAI radio said the worst was over.

Mayo and his trusted majordomo Porfirio Robles carried a straw basket and a strongbox full of wet cash to the little patio outside Robles's back door. Against the sandstone wall that protected the house from the street, the bougainvillea drooped into the mud, their usually brilliant blossoms faded and sodden, crushed by the rising water.

The heavy rains to the north and west had subsided before reaching Los Dos Laredos. The flooding of these Texas-Mexico border towns resulted from the overflowing Rio Grande, not from the skies.

The floodwaters drowned the bridge between Nuevo Laredo and Laredo, stranding Mayo at the Cadillac, so he had spent the night in the Mexican border city at Robles's modest home.

The men had been up for hours, tending to a wood fire on the back patio, drinking coffee at five, eating toasted, yeasty bolillos slathered with salty butter, watching the lightening sky and listening to the radio for the storm's next chapter.

Mayo trusted Henry Guerra, the San Antonio radio announcer who was a friend of his cousin Tony Bessan. If Henry Guerra said the weather was clearing, Mayo was ready to go back to work.

When first light hit the patio, Robles ascended first, climbing a ladder of uncertain stability up to the flat roof of his house. His *patrón,* Mayo, handed up the box and the basket and followed, his steps surprisingly spry for a sixty-nine-year-old man with a fear of heights.

In this July 1954 photo, flood damage is visible at the
busy Nuevo Laredo intersection of Ocampo and Bravo.

On that June morning in Nuevo Laredo, the post-dawn desert
heat was atypically heavy, steaming upward from the standing
water and drenched earth. By nine a.m., tar-paper roofs were shim-
mering. By lunchtime, it would be 100 humid degrees.

The roof was already hot to the touch as they set to work. Carefully peeling clumps of wet money apart, they laid out the soggy
bills into neat rows to roast in the dawning sun. The day before,
Mayo and Robles had waded downtown to the Cadillac, where
Mayo grabbed handfuls of soggy cash from the waterlogged safe.

This morning, from their vantage atop Robles's house, they
understood that Henry Guerra was wrong: The worst had just
begun. Looking north toward Laredo, the men saw that the international bridge was gone, swallowed by a river a mile wide.

The Rio Grande had claimed more than two hundred city
blocks in Laredo and an equivalent number in Nuevo Laredo. The
second-story roof of the *aduana*, the Mexican customs building,
was just visible in the roiling water. Miles away, houses and businesses were inundated as the flow backed up into the creeks.

Hundreds of blocks in both cities were underwater, ruined. No
electricity. No water.

I was four and a half. My sister Clay was three months old.

Our house was on the American side, in Laredo's old Montrose

More flood devastation is seen at Plaza Juárez in Nuevo Laredo in July 1954.

neighborhood near the river. We didn't have any close neighbors then, and from our backyard, we could see the ledge of the canyon where the often-dry Chacon Creek sometimes managed a mild trickle as it meandered through a deep gully 65 feet below.

On this day, El Chacón was a mighty river, eroding the ledge with its new fury. The roaring was scary enough to send me to my grandmother's arms. When our housekeeper, Micaela "Mickey" Mendoza, arrived and told us about seeing drowned horses and cattle in the floodwater, my father decided it was time to leave.

Across the river, in Nuevo Laredo, my grandfather stayed with Robles and his family for four days, drinking warm Coca-Cola and cooking over the fire on the patio after the power went out.

Our house in Laredo was never in danger, but because of my baby sister's needs, my mother and my maternal grandmother, Odette Bessan, packed us up and fled to our family's summer home in the Hill Country.

My father's mother, Lil Garner, and his sister, Jean Claire, who had just graduated from Laredo's Martin High School, headed to Cuero to stay with one of Lil's sisters.

This aerial view shows flooding in downtown and residential areas of Nuevo Laredo.

"Big Porter" Garner, my father's father, took command at the family compound, watching over the three houses, tending assorted pets and Odette's chickens. My father also stayed behind, awaiting marching orders from Mayo.

Mother said she remembers gagging at the stench of the inundated sewage treatment plant as she packed the Ford station wagon for our escape.

Ironically, as we retreated to our vacation home refuge in western Kerr County, near Hunt, we entered the zone of the storm, which in two days pounded the Devils River–Pecos Divide with thirty-eight inches of rain, water that headed down the Rio Grande.

What followed was the largest known flood along the Rio Grande in Texas, according to the federal agency that measures disasters. The impact on life and property was worse because the Amistad Dam wasn't finished until 1969. The dam was built near

Del Rio, upstream from Laredo at the confluence of the Rio Grande and the Devils River.

The floodwater destroyed the bridge in Eagle Pass and pushed heavy debris downriver to Laredo, where the fast-moving steel and concrete knocked out the railroad bridge and the city's only bridge into Mexico.

Six months earlier, the United States and Mexico had celebrated the dedication of the $50 million Falcon Dam project, about 75 miles downstream from Laredo on the Rio Grande. At its dedication, President Dwight Eisenhower and Mexican president Adolfo Ruiz Cortines officiated at what *Time* magazine called the largest joint border undertaking on record.

Today we talk about 100-year floods as the literal high-water mark of something terrible. Paleo-flood hydrologic studies of ancient Pecos River floods show that the 1954 flood was on the order of a 2,000-year event. That means the chance are 0.0005 percent of occurrence in a given year.

The rain started in Texas in the late morning of June 24, when Hurricane Alice left the Bay of Campeche and made landfall 20 miles south of Brownsville. The storm moved up the Rio Grande

DB-317—Rio Grande Flood of 1954, Laredo, Texas

Flooding looking south toward the Nuevo Laredo customs house.

Valley to the Devils River–Pecos Divide and rained hard and steady for a couple of days.

The US Geologic Survey says the flood stage in the Pecos River Canyon near Langtry exceeded 90 feet. In some areas, floodwater spilled out of the canyon onto the adjacent plateau.

Six days later, some 250 miles downstream in Laredo, the Rio Grande crested at 61.35 feet at 9:30 a.m. on June 30. The river was 15 feet above the washed-away international bridge. Damage was estimated to be approximately $113 million in today's dollars.

Mayo and Robles surveyed the devastation from the roof. As the water receded over the next few days, the muddy, rubble-strewn landscape scarcely resembled what had been their sprawling, bustling border towns.

Later they trudged from Robles's house through the smelly, murky water toward the central business district. Debris floated all around them: vegetation, broken wooden boxes, garbage and dishes, toys and dead animals.

Staggered by the destruction along the route to the Cadillac, they gasped in disbelief to see the bar's collapsed walls and broken entrance gate. Inside, it was worse, little to salvage in the restaurant, where the floodwaters had etched their signature on the painted columns in the middle of the main dining room.

Linen tablecloths wrapped grotesquely around overturned chairs. Highball glasses stuck out of the muck. The back-bar shelves were bare of bottles. Nothing.

The kitchen counters were coated in mud: plates and cups arranged in a filthy tableau crowned by heads of soggy lettuce.

Pancho Villa's saddle was gone.

Mayo and Robles didn't know it at the time, but just around the corner, the silver-studded saddle lay wedged against a utility pole in three feet of turgid water, victim of the deadliest flood in the history of the Texas-Mexico border.

Mayo Bessan's beloved Cadillac Bar had been swept away.

It would be almost a year before he and Robles served another Ramos gin fizz.

Porter Garner Jr.: *The International Boundary and Water Commission came within six inches of predicting the flood crest, but nobody believed them. It turned out to be the worst flood on the Rio Grande since 1932, when water got to the curb of the Cadillac.*

The night before, we stacked up everything we could at least table height and on the bar. I locked up and went home. The bridge was supposed to close at midnight. Mayo got up next morning early as usual and headed across the river. The water had not yet risen as high as the bridge, and he talked the customs men into letting him drive across.

So he ended up being over there during the flood, and he and Robles watched the water rise. He stayed at Robles's house for three days. On the fourth day, they allowed private plane owners to ferry passengers back and forth. I flew across, and he and Robles met me at the airport in Mayo's car.

Mayo had never flown and was reluctant to go up in the small plane. Robles and I conspired to get Mayo on the plane by appealing to his curiosity. We tricked him into testing the back seat, and the pilot took off. In the air Mayo asked how fast we were flying, and the pilot turned around and said, "About eighty-five miles an hour." With that, Mayo said, "You turn around and look where you're going." That was Mayo's only ride in an airplane

Wanda Bessan Garner: *There was no water. We couldn't wash Clay's diapers and there were no Pampers in those days. Chacon Creek was like a lake—dead horses floating by.*

Jean Claire Garner Turcotte: *Mother and I went to Aunt Jane's in Cuero. They were encouraging people to leave town. I didn't want to leave and miss all the excitement. It was just unreal to see that much water. The old Holding Institute school on the banks of the river was completely under water.*

Accounts in Nuevo Laredo's daily newspaper *El Mañana* describe the damage as more devastating on the Mexican side because of its lower elevation. More than a thousand homes were destroyed. The *centro* of the commercial district was hard hit, but there was no loss of life because of evacuation efforts by the Mexican army. The sewer plant overflowed, adding its virulent contents to tons of mud and debris.

Sara Puig Laas: *During the flood, there was no rain in Laredo—it was all upriver. In Laredo, it was blue skies and temperatures in the 100s. The water treatment plant was flooded, and drinking water was brought in on trucks. Anyone who had a water well had a line of friends outside their house, bringing their towels and shampoo and waiting for a chance to shower.*

I remember all traffic to and from Nuevo Laredo had to cross on the pontoon bridge until the bridge was rebuilt. My brother Larry and a lot of other students got jobs bailing water from the pontoon bridge. It was hot work, but they were glad to get it and did a worthwhile service keeping traffic going, although it was slow.

My first husband, Art Ochoa, and I were living in Falfurrias, but happened to be in Laredo during the flood. I remember watching the amazing water from my grandparents' house at 915 Zaragoza, across from San Agustín Church. They had two brick-walled terraces below the house level. The first was a rose garden, and the lower one was for barnyard animals, date palms, tools, etc. The old wooden door in the center of the high back wall opened to a broad carrizo and grass area leading to the river. That wall had withstood many river rampages before 1954, but since the previous flood, the customs people had built an inspection shed for trucks at riverbank level behind where La Posada Hotel stands today. If I remember correctly, it was a simple metal roof supported by metal poles.

As we watched from the top terrace, the water tore the shed from its concrete slab. The metal rooftop glimmered atop the water as it floated, in seeming slow motion, toward the high back wall. We watched it make soundless contact and veer off, leaving the wall to crumble before our eyes in the roiling water. The river eventually came within three inches of the top terrace (yes, Grandpa measured it) before it began to back off.

Until the US Army Corps of Engineers built the pontoon bridge, the only way to get to New Laredo was to fly across. Then you had to

A pontoon bridge built by the US Army Corps of Engineers crossed the Rio Grande while the new, permanent bridge was under construction, 1954. Author's collection.

go to the Mexican army garrison to get a permit to enter the flood zone for daylight-only access. Soldiers, focused on preventing looting, retrieved Pancho Villa's saddle from a guy carrying it on his back.

Four days after the June 1954 flood, the Corps of Engineers installed a one-lane rubber pontoon bridge. Some eighteen days later, the Laredo Bridge System replaced that bridge with a stronger two-lane wooden pontoon bridge that allowed international traffic to return to near normal and toll collections to resume.

Penny Gallahan Cornelius: *The pontoon bridge the Army Corps of Engineers built was anchored on the US side for a while by my father's big winch truck. He lived in the truck for the duration of its use, and we would take him food there so he wouldn't have to leave. I was small and afraid the river would swallow the truck if the water didn't soon subside.*

About two years later, the pontoon bridge was replaced with a four-lane pre-stressed concrete bridge with pedestrian sidewalks and aluminum railings. Designed by engineers from the Mexican government, with consulting engineers in Laredo, the bridge was rated as the "most modern" bridge on the Pan-American Highway.

Porter: *It took a while to decide whether we would reopen. The building was ruined and so much was lost. The employees came back and worked hard, cleaning and sifting through the mud. We* *worked about four weeks salvaging things. We managed to save a lot, pots and pans, and we stored things as best we could.*

Ultimately, the building's landlord paid for the repairs, but Mayo and Porter had to resupply everything else. The arrangement allowed the Cadillac to modernize and put in air conditioning, which Mayo had resisted because of the expense.

Almost nine months to the day after the flood, the Cadillac reopened on April 1, 1954, with central air and heat, a new bar, new bathrooms, and a fenced parking lot.

Imagine today's costs of setting up a restaurant from scratch.

Meeting Up at the Cadillac

Just as oil came to define the Texas economy beginning in the early twentieth century, Laredo and the surrounding counties became well known then, as now, for a bounty of oil and gas.

In 1921, O. W. Killam brought the boom to Mirando City, about 45 miles east of Laredo. When Killam started the South Texas oil boom, people were flaring natural gas because there was no use for it. In the 1970s, descendants of those early oil millionaires hit another gusher when natural gas became the most-sought-after natural resource.

The Mirando City boom boosted the once agriculturally dominated economy in Laredo, giving rise to new banks and businesses: the Laredo National and the Union National; Richter's Department Store; new hotels, the Plaza and the Hamilton; and the Plaza Theatre. Mercy Hospital, remodeled from the old Steffian home on Jarvis Plaza, expanded to a modern three-story building.

In 1930, the first antimony plant was built on the north outskirts of town by Texas Mining & Smelting, a European company that first operated in San Luis Potosí, Mexico, and then moved to Laredo.

With the expansion of the Pan-American Highway, international commerce made the border towns thriving ports of entry. Brokerage houses and warehouses were built, and Laredo became the headquarters for the 23rd US Customs Collection District.

Laredo began to exploit its connections south of the border, capitalizing on being the Gateway to Mexico, replacing its previous claim as the Bermuda Onion Capital of the World.

Killam became a community leader and served as president of the Laredo Chamber of Commerce. It was his idea to invite Texas

Mayo and Odette's only child, Wanda Mae, was part of the 1931 Washington's Birthday parade. She is seated at top, wearing a bonnet.

lawmakers and politicians to Laredo for the annual Washington's Birthday Celebration, in what became a tradition of schmoozing that continues today, attracting all the big-name elected officials in the state.

In a history of the Washington Birthday Celebration, Killam's son, Radcliffe, said his father wanted the state to build a highway from Laredo to Mirando City, so in 1924 he leased a train, invited Lieutenant Governor T. W. Davidson and members of the Texas House and Senate, and showed them a good time on both sides of the Rio Grande.

Laredo's improbable observance of George Washington's birthday began in 1898 as a celebration by a civic club improbably known as the Improved Order of Red Men, part of a late nineteenth century trend that saw a rise in fraternal organizations across America. Seeking a holiday to unite the border communities, the group settled on honoring George Washington, who was admired in both the United States and Mexico. The one-off celebration evolved into an annual multiday cross-cultural observance on both sides of the Rio Grande, with a colonial pageant and fancy-dress debutante ball, sporting events, a jalapeño-eating contest, and a ceremony at the midpoint of the main international bridge featuring *abrazo* children representing both countries.

As the Cadillac acquired a reputation for good drinks and fine food, it also became the meeting point for politicians during the annual Washington Birthday events. It was said, only half jokingly, that every February the state capital moved to Laredo.

State and national leaders from the United States and Mexico seized the opportunity for valuable face time in a social setting, and lobbyists were only too happy to pick up the tab.

All the state bigwigs passed through the Cadillac. Governors from Dan Moody to Bill Clements to Ann Richards, including George W. Bush before he was governor and Rick Perry when he was still in the legislature.

Porter: *One year we had five governors—from Texas, New Mexico, and three from Mexico. I can't remember a year when the Texas governor and lieutenant governor didn't come to the Cadillac during the celebration. People would be standing on the sidewalk when we opened. On most weekends, but especially during February, the bridge was bumper to bumper as people waited sometimes for more than an hour to get across the river. It was almost impossible to get*

The author sported her cowgirl outfit at Washington's Birthday Celebration parade in February 1954. On the float above her, her aunt Jean Claire Garner makes her bow as a Society of Martha Washington debutante.

back and forth across the bridge except by walking."

Politicos from Austin mingled with constituents, more worried about their next tequila sour than the highway appropriation vote on Monday.

A keen observer of this phenomenon at the state and national level was Austin political adviser Tony Proffitt, whose career spanned work for Congressman Jake Pickle and assignments for the LBJ White House and many Texas lawmakers, most notably as press secretary to Lieutenant Governor Bob Bullock. The Washington Birthday Celebration Association honored Bullock as Mr. South Texas in 1993. Governor Ann Richards got the award in 1994.

Tony Proffitt: *Laredo and Washington's birthday was on everybody's calendar. Pickle loved going down there, and so did Bill Hobby, Ann Richards, and Bullock, too. There was probably more state business conducted at the Cadillac than anyone realized.*

A crowd swelled the bar during this Washington's Birthday celebration in 1937, including Albert Martin, Joe "Pepe" Martin, and Matias De Llano.

Revelers raise their glasses during the 1937 George Washington's Birthday Celebration.

Even during the Depression years, business leaders made special efforts to keep the lawmakers coming. In 1932, Ed Corrigan, president of the Washington Birthday Celebration, insisted that the festivities go on. That year Corrigan supervised the parade from the sidecar of a motorcycle.

Among those who heeded Corrigan's invitation to visit Laredo was John Nance "Cactus Jack" Garner, soon to be elected vice president of the United States. Garner was a cousin of my grandfather, Porter Sr. In the fifties, Cactus Jack's son, Tully, was the US customs collector in Laredo.

After the Depression, Washington's Birthday weekend revelry returned in full force. At the Cadillac, tourists competed with the locals for tables and elbow room at the bar. Hail-fellow-well-met prevailed, and they were all one another's new best friend.

In a prime people-watching corner, the old-timers huddled, surveying the year's crop of debs and frat boys, unleashed and drinking fifty-cent cocktails poured with premium whiskey. Older Laredo customers typically avoided Nuevo Laredo during Washington's Birthday weekend, but the town's hard drinkers were there when the bar opened at ten o'clock each morning. Sometimes they'd go home for a nap and return for the evening shift, tippling and swapping tales until my grandfather started his poker game in the back room, or in later years, when my father would turn out the lights and send them home to their families.

My mother remembers a story from Mayo's days at the Cadillac, when Al Roschuni worked the closing shift during the Washington's birthday celebration.

Wanda Bessan Garner: *A drunk woman customer got boisterous and unruly. When Al refused to serve her, she sat down on the floor in front of the bar. Al picked her up by the nape of her mink coat and dragged her out the front door and locked it.*

The first Oil Scouts reunion attracted about thirty-five people, including a few landmen and the local oil community. Hooton, Milton "Doc" Adams, and George Buck got it organized and put together a golf tournament at Lake Casablanca. The next year, more than a hundred people showed up.

The Cadillac was always a popular venue for ladies' luncheons; here a circa 1960s meeting of the board of directors of the Martha Washington Society. From left, seated Frances Sulak, Louise Puig, Grace Milton, Wanda Bessan Garner, Patsy Foster Moore (behind the flowers), and Sheila Slaughter Glassford. Standing: Ann Neel, Angie Borchers, Liz Foster, Leona Alston, Julie Watson, Idalia Richter, Patsy Brand Sanditen, and Olga Rosenbaum Meyer.

Through the years, the back room was a favored poker spot for the oil scouts who frequented the area, chasing Killam's boom that created new fortunes for old families in Webb and Zapata Counties.

Decades later, the Cadillac remained the popular watering hole of these landmen, and every Monday night they would arrive for drinks and dinner and do an informal "check," sharing their reports of actual and potential drilling.

Among my father's favorites was Jim Hooton, who lived in Corpus Christi and worked for Humble Oil. His son was Burt Hooton, who pitched for UT and for the Dodgers.

Porter: *I'd gotten to know 'em over the years. They'd sit in the back room and play liar's poker, with dollar-bill serial numbers. If you lost, you had to give everybody at the table a dollar.*

Years later, Jim Hooton and my father would reminisce about their pals, eventually leading to the first of many reunions. Styled as

Longtime friends and regular customers, the Horace Hall family, 1959.

the old scouts roundup, the evening cost $5 a head and covered anything they wanted to eat and drink between seven and ten p.m.

The first reunion in the early seventies attracted about thirty-five people, including a few landmen and the local oil community. Hooton, Milton "Doc" Adams, and George Buck got it organized and also put together a golf tournament at Lake Casablanca. The next year, more than a hundred people showed up. The oil scouts roundup eventually outgrew the Cadillac and moved to the Laredo Country Club.

Jason L. Kuenstler: *To me as a young petroleum landman cutting my teeth in South Texas, there was nothing more exciting than working the border towns, and Laredo was the crème de la crème. So many great memories at the Cadillac, wild and fun times with friends and coworkers and later many, many great times and memories with my wife. The annual Laredo oil scouts roundup was never complete without a night at the Cadillac. Those were the days! Unfortunately, from an industry standpoint, we now have a whole generation of young landmen who don't understand the draw of* *working South Texas. Really sad what has happened in Mexico, so many good people hurt. Glad I had the opportunity to know it when I did.*

After the flood, the remodeled rear dining room was the chosen spot for special occasions and ladies' luncheons. The waiters would push the tables together, set out the homemade hot sauce and bolillos, and wait for Laredo's distaff aristocracy to arrive for what regularly turned into a four-hour lunch.

Sometimes it would be a birthday party, with the ladies at one long table, flanked by a table laden with presents wrapped and tied and identified with shiny stickers from Deutsch's, the Bon-Ton, or Milton's Jewelers, Richter's, and later, Polly Adams and Le Passe.

When the time came to open the gifts, an overabundance of tequila sours and gin fizzes blurred the design on the silk scarves

NUEVO LAREDO MEXICO

When Jean Claire, far right, graduated from high school in May 1954, she had a graduation party at the Cadillac, including Peggy Cullinan, Yvonne Sulak, Lynn Taylor, Ellen Taylor, Annette McCauley, and Mary Jo Watt.

and engraved cigarette cases. My father would send over coffee, and the ladies would try to sober up in time to pick up their children at school.

Saturday night and Sunday lunch brought the locals to the table.

Tom Deliganis Jr: *I recall going to the Cadillac every Sunday after church. I also took my prom date there, and we ate cabrito. I've tried to relate that to my non-Laredo friends. "Yes, I took my date to a foreign country so we could eat goat." They just don't understand.*

One regular group included Laredo mayor Hugh Cluck and his wife, Emmie, Albert and Agnes Martin, and sometimes Horace and Mary Paul Hall.

Porter: *The waiter would take the drink orders at the Clucks' table and Hugh would decline, but then Hugh would excuse himself to the men's room and drink doubles in the hallway. The waiters knew the drill and served his drinks there.*

Like clockwork, fifteen minutes after The Lawrence Welk Show *went off, the Slaughter family walked in: Dave and Offye, and Dave's brother. Randolph Slaughter, who later married Lilia Bruni. Julie Bell and Truman Phelps were usually with them.*

Marcus Wormser loved cabrito, never ordered anything else, but he always wanted his refried beans on a separate plate. The first

Saturday was local night at the Cadillac as friends table-hopped, sharing drinks and appetizers, nachos or maybe chicken guacamole. Shown here are two couples who were close friends to Wanda and Porter Garner: Barbara and Bill Powell and Edgar and Annie Mims, 1965.

We all met at the Cadillac Bar on spring break.

Porter welcomed college students on spring break unless the boys' hair was too long and shaggy or the girls' skirts were too short. This group passed the Cadillac dress code. Shown seated, center: Christie Barrera and Louise Mandel. Glen Jackson is holding the piñata and Janice Fitzgibbon-Hughes is standing to his right. Photo from the collection of Janice Fitzgibbon-Hughes.

thing he did was to cover them with sugar and stir it up while they were good and hot, and then he ate the beans for dessert. We never served desserts because we wanted to serve those after-dinner drinks, crème de menthe and grasshoppers and brandy.

My brother Bubba, more formally known as Porter S. Garner III, graduated from Texas A&M the week before the Cadillac closed in 1979. Growing up as the last child at home after my sister and I went off to college, "little" Porter often accompanied our father across the river. He soon realized that "big" Porter had a long to-do list.

Porter Garner III: *My earliest memories of the Cadillac Bar involve me getting up early in the morning and going to work with my dad. He always wanted to be there before six a.m., and he would put me to work immediately.*

Much of the work he assigned me at the Cadillac was probably busywork, likely intended to instill a work ethic and a discipline in me. And if you don't think cleaning and shining a thirty-foot-long brass footrail, emptying out and cleaning brass spittoons, and washing base tile all around the floors instills a work ethic in you, you'll just have to trust me, it does. I always knew my dad was loving and caring, but as I grew older, I realized just how dedicated he was to me and my future. In fact, the next summer I graduated to working in the bodega, alongside Chango, squeezing limes, chipping ice, and hauling cases of beer and liquor to the bar. This seemed like a promotion.

Although I didn't realize it then, those were good times and now represent great memories.

After Porter III graduated from Texas A&M, he worked for the Hughes Tool Company before joining the Association of Former Students in 1981 as field director. In 2000, he was named president and CEO of the association.

Porter III: *My dad and I were very close until the day he died, and I miss him daily. I attribute much of my success in life to the values he instilled in me while working and learning from him. As I reflect*

After Porter III graduated from Texas A&M University in 1979, friends and family gathered for a celebration in Aggieland. Shown here: Porter Jr., Class of '45; Porter III; and TAMU Dean of Admissions Ed Cooper. Porter III is the executive director of the Association of Former Students at A&M. From the author's personal collection.

Porter S. Garner Jr. and Porter S. Garner III in 2000, shortly after Porter III became president and CEO of the Association of Former Students. Photo from the collection of Porter S. Garner III.

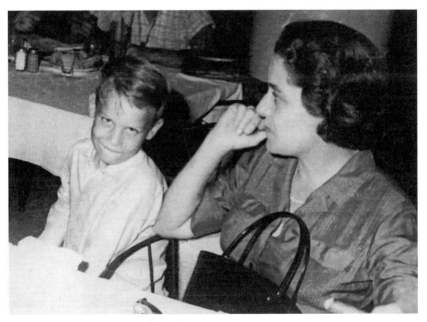

Porter III and his mother Wanda.

on my memories of the Cadillac Bar, and the time spent with my dad, I cherish those memories even more.

My sister, Clay Garner Berry, was fifteen when Mayo Bessan died, but she keeps his and Porter's legacy alive for her daughter, Blake Berry.

Clay Garner Berry: *My memories of the Cadillac are heartfelt, from countless birthday parties, and Washington's Birthday Celebrations, dinners with special friends, and those favorable (and sometimes unfavorable) dates.*

Needless to say, the waiters were like our family, and they were good at keeping secret the number of cocktails we enjoyed. That is, until Dad saw the tab. He would ask if we enjoyed ourselves, because our bar bill was considerably higher than the food bill. But he never seemed bothered by it.

⇉7⇇

The Party's Over

Sunday, December 2, 1979.

The last night of the Cadillac Bar, my husband, Richard, and I drove across the river with my father to help load up the things we wanted to save: Pancho Villa's silver-trimmed saddle, the carnival sideshow mirror that distorted your reflection, some cook pots from the kitchen, ancient mirrors bought a half century earlier in New Orleans antique shops.

And an armload of photos made by a photographer who made his living off tourists looking for proof they'd gotten drunk in Mexico. Pictures of legendary bartenders, long-dead celebrities, football players, family and friends who sought refuge and refreshments at the Cadillac.

We pulled into the empty parking lot a little after ten, having waited until we knew the staff had cleared out. Dad unlocked the kitchen door, and we walked past the hallway to the men's room, around the ancient ice-grinding machine that rendered fifty-pound blocks of ice into chips for the bar, and through the swinging doors into the main dining room.

The restaurant was eerily quiet, but it looked like business as usual: glasses polished and gleaming on the bar, floors swept and mopped, ready for the next day's round of drinks and dishes. The wooden kitchen counters were still damp from the end-of-shift scrubbing.

We were somber as Dad pointed out what he wanted to keep.

He was grim-faced, and I knew he was sad. But he approached the end of the Cadillac in his usual way, organized and orderly, just as he lived the rest of his life.

Kitchen counters on the last night of the Cadillac Bar were scrubbed and ready for the next day's opening.

In the darkened room, a tiny spotlight illuminated my grandfather's portrait, which had hung behind the long oak bar for all of my life. It was an old-fashioned formal pose, taken some time in the 1930s. Mayo looked straight ahead, his right arm resting on a podium of some sort, his gaze beyond the camera.

We remember people the way they looked the last time you saw them. I guess this is the mind's trick to ease the unsettling visual evidence of passing time. But I remember my grandfather as the young man in that portrait, although he was nearly sixty years old when I was born in 1949.

Mayo Bessan was always larger than life, never seeming old, though he was eighty-five when he died after a stroke in 1970. My family's oral history and the scrapbooks that document it are vivid enlargements of the slight gray-haired man I knew as my "Big Daddy."

As Richard lifted my grandfather's picture off its hook, my father stood on the public side of the bar, casting a sideways glance and frowning as though he had taken a blow.

There they were, Mayo and Porter: the beginning and the end of a love affair with the border that spanned more than fifty years. Like some love stories, this one was tender and enduring. Like others, it was sad, turbulent, and often unrequited.

Porter: *I was there a little over thirty-three years. I had a lot of fun. Made a lot of friends. But I hated dealing with the Mexican government and the union. It was time to go and I was ready. The only thing I've missed are my friends.*

That last night, we walked through the dining room in uneasy silence, my father's limping gait swooshing on the terrazzo floor. This silent place, usually so rambunctious with people having a good time, drinking and eating, was resting for the next day's business. Tables and cocktail shakers set up in silent anticipation of the next day's old friends and their older jokes.

I stood next to the kitchen doorway, looking out over the big dining room from my father's usual vantage point at the little table next to the hulking iron safe. I tried to imagine the scenes he had directed, the fights he had refereed, the revelry he had presided over for more than thirty years.

I glanced at my father and wondered whether he was remembering the hard times of slow business, air conditioning broken down in July, government interference by corrupt Mexican bureaucrats, or gunplay in the crosstown drug wars that wounded the

Porter's farewell to the Cadillac, last time he stood behind the bar, December 2, 1979. Author's personal collection.

Cadillac's top cook, "Colorado" Contreras, as he lay sleeping in his bed.

Porter: *What happened in Nuevo Laredo with the drug cartels is much more serious than what Mexico experienced during the 1970s. Back then, a family on the outskirts of Nuevo Laredo had the drug operation. A downtown nightclub had its share of incidents, shootings. But the criminal activity mostly occurred in the wee hours and had very little effect on tourism. The army finally went out to the dope house and in a pitched battle took care of the problem. Mexico City sent a man to oversee the interdiction. He and his team stayed in Laredo at the Hamilton Hotel.*

President Richard Nixon blamed Mexico for the drug abuse problem in the United States, believing that marijuana and heroin were crossing the porous border and contaminating American cities. Following a report by Nixon's task force on drugs, the White House in September 1969 launched "Operation Intercept" at the US-Mexico border,

It was a short-lived effort that cost upward of $30 million, without any significant drug seizures, according to Helen Redmond in her 2011 article, "The Political Economy of Mexico's Drug War." Crossing the border became an hours-long ordeal as the administration stationed an additional 2,000 US customs and border patrol agents to stop and search every vehicle.

Thousands of people, Mexicans and Americans, were strip-searched, and traffic at the border backed up for miles, Trade between the two countries was effectively halted, border economies collapsed, and thousands of Mexicans lost their jobs, Redmond writes.

Three weeks after the interdiction began, the United States quietly withdrew the border drug agents.

The effects in Laredo were mainly felt in what could be a five-to-six-hour wait to cross the bridge.

Over the years, the Cadillac's biggest financial hits came during the Cuban missile crisis and after President John Kennedy's assassination.

Porter: *In the fall of 1962, there was no tourism. Everyone knew America was on the edge of something bad happening. The least wrong move could have put us in all-out nuclear war. Everybody was scared to death. A year later, after Kennedy was assassinated, things tightened on the bridge for a few weeks and business almost came to a stop.*

I'd go out to Lake Casablanca and hit a golf ball and worry to death, and then I'd hit another one.

In 1979, closing the Cadillac had been a family topic for months, as my father pondered a life away from Mexico, far from the strikes and bribes and corruption.

Porter: *Even though I had all the permits and licenses required, it seemed like they always wanted one more thing. There was an inspector for everything. One time an inspector fined me for having matches behind the bar. He said I had to have a special permit. I had to pay a "fee," a mordida.*

Dad planned to give the keys and the business to his employees and just walk away. He only leased the property from Octaviano "Chito" Longoria, and there was no possibility of the children continuing the business and no thought of selling it.

He had consulted with the labor union officials earlier in the week, and on Monday morning, he met with José María Morelos, head of the Nuevo Laredo waiters union, and officials at the Nuevo Laredo arbitration board, and signed an agreement declaring the business officially closed. In the agreement, he turned over all furnishings and equipment to the waiters union.

Porter: *In recent years, I had closed down for a week at Christmas to get all the employee vacations taken care of at one time. So I decided if I was going to close the business, that would be a good time to do it. The night before we were going to close, I didn't even tell Elias about it and closed up just as usual for vacation.*

Jean Claire Garner Turcotte and Porter at the farewell lunch.

Tuesday morning, key employees, the Cadillac's manager Elias Álvarez, and Rocha, the union representative, met with Dad at a bank in Laredo. Vacation time and bonuses were paid. The lease was paid up for six months. Dad said he was giving the business to the employees, but they didn't really understand. Rocha immediately spoke up to say what the union would do, but my father said the union didn't have anything to do with the deal. The Cadillac belonged to the employees, and now they were the *patrones*.

The employees struggled to keep the Cadillac going, but faced insurmountable odds.

After about six months, the business was taken over by Don Octaviano Longoria's grandson, Ramón Salido Jr. and his great-grandson O. L. "Chitito" Longoria. They operated the business until September 1991, when the cousins feuded and effectively split the Cadillac into two businesses. The Longoria cousin took the original venue and renamed it El Dorado Bar, while the Salido family moved the Cadillac Bar to a new address on Calle Victoria.

Ramón Salido presided over a faithful re-creation, down to the embroidered napkins, the menu, and even the bartenders mixing the Ramos gin fizzes. The only jarring note was an offtrack betting operation in an adjoining space. But then, Mayo probably would have approved.

But in 2004, business began its irrevocable slide in Nuevo Laredo as violence escalated among the warring drug cartels. The final iteration of the Cadillac Bar in Nuevo Laredo closed in 2010.

Writing in the *San Antonio Express-News* in December 2010, John MacCormack noted that almost all "the venerable Nuevo Laredo tourist destinations—from the cabrito place El Rincon Del Viejo to the Cadillac Bar to Marti's Gift Shop—are closed. Only a few bars remain open in the downtown, all operating under the heavy boot heel of the Zetas."

By 2016, Tilman Fertitta, billionaire owner of the Landry's restaurant empire, owned four Cadillac Bar locations: in Las Vegas, Houston, Kemah, and Lake Charles.

Separately owned Cadillac Bars also operate in San Antonio and San Francisco.

At these outposts, the logos, the menus, and even some of the recipes mimic Mayo Bessan's original Cadillac Bar, once dubbed by *The New York Times* as the "best run and most delightful watering hole" on the US-Mexico border.

But none ever captured Mayo and Porter's comfortable and cordial creation, "Where Old Friends Meet."

Porter and his first grandson, Austin Garner Cash, at the farewell lunch.

That last night at the Cadillac Bar, we packed my father's truck and our car with sentimental mementos and practical kitchen equipment.

In his retirement home in the Hill Country, my father used the thirty-gallon cook pot to make wine sauce each fall, straining the meaty mixture through a china cap sieve from the Cadillac. He had his cabrito pan, chef's knives, and saucepans, boxes of plastic spoons and cocktail picks, waiter's jackets and napkins with *Cadillac Bar* embroidered in the signature red thread.

Pancho Villa's saddle sits on a wooden mount in our home. Most times, during a party or dinner, visitors will climb on and have a picture taken. Ramos gin fizzes might be involved.

≫8≪

Recipes from the Cadillac

Signs proclaiming *We're from New Orleans* and *Famous Ramos Gin Fizz*, welcomed customers from across the Rio Grande to the Cadillac. Mexican food was on the menu, but so were frog legs and green turtle soup made from scratch.

Veteran waiter Francisco Segovia attends to our family lunch, probably in late December 1953. This could have been the occasion when the author threw a fit and bit through her water glass leaving a permanent scar on her upper lip.

The cooks at the Cadillac stirred up a menu from a Cajun/Cre-ole/Tex-Mex melting pot.

Beef tacos? *Seguro que sí.*

Snapper en papillote? *Bien sûr.*

Mayo and Odette Bessan came from families in southern Louisiana where cooking is a genetically inherited trait. In Arcadian "Cajun" country, you were measured by how well you could make a roux, tell a joke, and bluff a winning poker pot with a pair of nines.

Food, storytelling, and card playing were the social gauges.

But if shrewd cardsmanship was strutting stuff, being able to choose the best hen for a chicken stew was even more admired.

Besides eating good food, my Louisiana kin liked to talk about food, even more than they enjoyed telling jokes about one another. It was part of the dynamic for host and guests to compare recipes and then shrug or boast about their own accomplishments, passing dish after dish around the table.

I learned to cook in my grandmother Odette's kitchen, absorbing her intuitive methods for presentation and seasoning, from pungent chile pequins to flowery filé powder (sassafras).

Pinches, dashes, a cup filled to "about here." Water filled the pot to the second knuckle for white rice. This was part of her heritage, and it became mine, too, as I fed my college friends from her recipes and continue today to feel happiest in the kitchen or basking at the table at the end of a meal.

The Cadillac never had shrimp gumbo on the menu, but many other menu items were flavored with the tastes Mayo and Odette grew up with.

In the Cadillac kitchen, Mayo imported that country goodness based on backyard gardens, fat chickens, and brown Gulf shrimp, and then added what he'd learned during his bachelor days waiting tables in New Orleans's best restaurants: the lagniappes of rich or piquant sauces, fancy garnishes and fancier drinks, the little exotic touches of trout cooked in a parchment bag and tiny lake shrimp in a creamy remoulade served over julienned lettuce.

Translating Louisiana bayou cooking to the dusty Mexican border during Prohibition took a bit of doing. Mayo used seafood imported from New Orleans and Tampico, and the translation

Family lunch, pre-flood, spring 1954. The author, Porter, Lil Garner, Odette Bessan, Mayo Bessan, Jean Claire Garner, Wanda Garner, and Porter Garner Sr.

worked to delight the Cadillac customers, enchanted at the departure from Tex-Mex and amazed by the kitchen's seafood wizardry.

And the salads! Whoever had seen so many different kinds of salads in a frontier town? Why, you could make a meal on guacamole and the salads then known with the politically incorrect names of the wop and the dago.

Later, Mayo and his cooks capitalized on the similarities between the staple dishes in Mexican cooking and the French and Creole dishes he grew up on, baked, smothered, fricasseed.

While Mayo was every inch a showman, he knew the best food was simply prepared, and he kept his menus basic and straightforward.

Good steaks, the best seafood he could import from Bagille's, the legendary fish wholesaler in New Orleans, bolillos made fresh daily from an old French bread recipe, and strong whiskey filled the Cadillac's larder.

Mayo wasn't a cook, but he grew up surrounded by cooks in New Iberia and later in New Orleans, forming definite opinions about laying out a table.

Porter: *Mayo knew what he liked. For a while he had a cook named Sardina, who later opened his own place. After that, Mayo* *made a deal with Pete Coussoulis to run the restaurant operation while Mayo ran the bar. After Mayo bought out Pete, another Cajun friend, Al Roschuni, ran the kitchen and taught the Mexican cooks how to cook French and Creole food. Al brought recipes with him: turtle soup and shrimp Louisiane, the dressings for dago and wop salads, wine sauce and trout en papillote.*

The Cadillac kitchen was founded on recipes from Mayo's extended south Louisiana family: Bessan, Savoie, Theriot, Courtois, and Daigre. He styled the presentations and flourishes after such places as Galatoire's, where he had a brief stint as a waiter not long after that fabled restaurant opened, and long-gone eateries in the old Tenderloin District, where he tended bar in a time when Louis Armstrong was a kid singing on street corners and learning to play the cornet.

New Iberia formed his cook's appetite. New Orleans created his showman's soul.

Regular Cadillac customers had their favorite waiters, who had drinks on the table by the time they sat down. Among them were Francisco "Pancho" Segovia, Manuel Tapia, and Salome Montes.

The maître d's over the years included Domingo Falciola, Hilario Mejia, and the beloved Porfirio Robles, at whose deathbed my grandfather kept vigil.

Presiding at the bar were Eduardo Rodríguez, Sixto Sánchez, and Pancho Díaz. Wearing starched, pristine white jackets with the red stitched *Cadillac* over the left breast, they stood proud and courtly, keeping the drinks flowing and making sure the drunks went somewhere else.

Elias Álvarez, who would eventually become a manager at the Cadillac, first became acquainted with Mayo and Porter when he worked for the Carta Blanca distributorship across the street from the Cadillac on Belden.

Álvarez wanted to immigrate to the United States and needed a job, so he went to work at the locker plant Porter Sr. owned in Laredo until Porter Jr. needed him at the Cadillac.

Porter: *Elias Álvarez was kind of a jack-of-all-trades. He was a fine man of great integrity. He was my eyes at the Cadillac.*

The other rich concoction invented in the Cadillac's kitchen was the wine sauce, ladled generously over bacon-wrapped filet mignon, quail, and dove.

Porter: *A very nice gentleman named Polo Quintana, who lived not too far from the Cadillac, had a ranch outside Nuevo Laredo and was kind enough to let us go white-winged dove hunting any time we wanted to. Al and I shot most of the doves we served at the Cadillac. It was not unusual for us to shoot a hundred birds in an afternoon. We'd take the shoeshine boys to shag the birds.*

Over the years, the kitchen crew and the waitstaff stayed mostly the same, with little turnover. When the Cadillac closed in 1979, there were thirty-two employees, and the average tenure was eighteen years.

Porter: *Our cooks knew how to make our dishes, and that's it. I would hire them in as dishwashers and then train them to cook. The dishwasher immediately started learning how to be a salad man, who was already learning how to be a cook. We always had somebody ready to take over.*

José Torres was our oldest longtime cook, along with Librado Tijerina and "Colorado" Contreras.

The biggest sellers were the filet and the cabrito, but the kitchen also turned out a lot of Mexican food: chicken envueltos, enchiladas, beef tacos. The seafood dishes were always a crowd favorite, trout broiled whole or en papillote, crab and shrimp, sauced and baked and fried frog legs.

Porter: *We ordered most of our seafood from Bagille's in New Orleans: crabmeat and soft-shelled crabs, turtle meat, flounder, lobsters, scallops, oysters, and horseradish roots to make cocktail sauce and other sauces. All the difference in the world to use fresh grated horseradish.*

It would come from New Orleans on the Southern Pacific evening train and arrive in San Antonio about ten the next morning. A

Employees and their families at the annual Cadillac Christmas party, 1965

Railway Express truck would pick it up and take it to the Missouri Pacific station. It got to Laredo that afternoon, less than twenty-four hours after I placed the order.

Fish were broiled on a griddle. Put a little grease on the griddle, put the fish on top of it, and cover the fish with a china plate. Turn it over and finish it. Put it on a platter and top it with melted butter, lime juice, and finely chopped parsley. The challenge was getting a whole fish that was the right size. Getting a uniform size, 1 1/8 pounds, was difficult to come by.

Here Porter shrugs off the unforgettable fried shrimp:

Porter: *Nothing to it. Flour, milk, and egg batter. Shrimp were already boiled, ready to eat. That way we could fry them quickly without having to worry about whether the shrimp were done. We dipped the shrimp in batter and that was it.*

Fish en papillote was a labor-intensive dish that took a lot of time. Originally we used pompano, but it priced itself out of the market and then got so they couldn't give it away. We used snapper,

flounder, and trout. Trout wasn't the best because it is such a deli-
cate flesh. Snapper did better.

We parboiled the fish filets first. Made a béchamel sauce with
shrimp, crabmeat, and white wine. Take the paper sack; rub the
entire inside with oil. Lay two filets and spoon the sauce over it.
Roll the end of the sack tightly to keep the air out. Put it on a plate
and cook it in the oven. At the table, the waiter would use scissors
to snip the sack, fold it open, spoon some out, and close the sack
until next serving was needed.

For decades, the frog legs came from Rayne, Louisiana, where a
trio of Parisians, Jacques Weil and his brothers, began a profit-
able business, shipping the butchered bullfrogs across the United
States and to gourmet restaurants in France. Rayne, long known as
the frog capital of the world, still has an annual frog festival.

Later, the snapper and frog legs and turtle meat came from
Tampico, and then from the west coast of Mexico. My father said

In 1945, a full dinner went for 75 cents, including an appetizer,
an entrée, and a salad. Diners could choose à la carte, selecting
from a shrimp or oyster cocktail for $1, shrimp à la Louisiane for
$1.75, or guacamole for 70 cents.

Five years later, the high-dollar
entrees included filet mignon in wine
sauce for $1.75, and snapper en papil-
lote and lobster Newburg for $2.25.

Tables were set with white cloths
and napkins, with *Cadillac Bar* embroidered on them in red. Straw baskets
held saltine crackers to dip into the
salsa cruda made fresh each morning.

In those days, fried tortilla chips
were a rarity. Only the guacamole
salad and refried beans included the
homemade totopos or tostadas. Even
the rich, gooey chile con queso was
served with toast points or warm corn
tortillas.

Cadillac menu, 1945

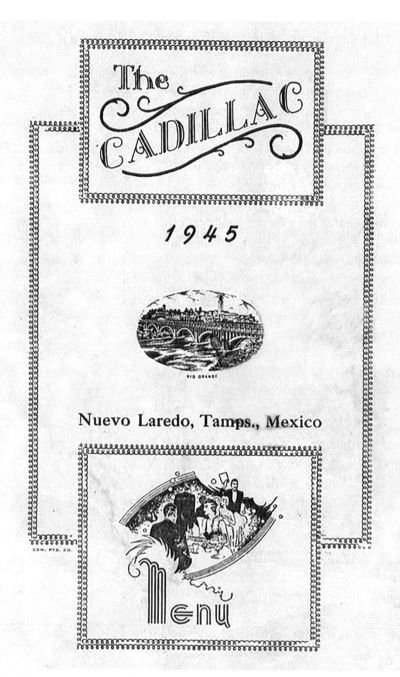

The CADILLAC

1945

RIO GRANDE

Nuevo Laredo, Tamps., Mexico

Menu

Cadillac menu cover, 1945.

Porter: *We served nachos at the Cadillac, but they weren't on the menu. You had to know to ask for them. Just tostadas, cheese, and jalapeño slices. Nothing else fancy. We also made our own potato chips and waffle chips on a mandoline. They were great. Matter of fact, I don't know of anything over there that wasn't good.*

We would cut our own filets from the big loin and wrapped them in bacon. With the leftover tips and trimmings, we'd make a stew for the kitchen staff and waiters. We didn't serve it to customers. You can make it all kinds of ways, but we'd make it with tomato paste, onions, potato, and seasoning, little chile serrano for flavor and heat. Salt and pepper, of course.

With your meal, the waiter delivered a basket of linen-swathed bolillos, the delectable mini loaves of French bread, warm and yeasty with a dusting of flour left over from the baking oven.

Porter: *I bought the bolillos from a fellow named Almanza, who really wanted to make only the big loaves because the little ones were hard to make. So I paid him the price of the big loaves. They were delivered in big straw baskets at eleven-thirty every morning. And when they came in hot and fresh, I'd put real butter on them, and man, were they good.*

On weekends, people who came down from San Antonio wanted some to take home. It wasn't anything to have a hundred dozen bolillos ordered for people to carry away.

As an antidote to the arid days and nights, Mayo and the bartenders mixed fancy drinks: tequila and whiskey sours, martinis, Planter's punch, stingers, Sazeracs, sidecars, old-fashioneds, and of course, the New Orleans or Ramos gin fizz, a "sissy" drink with milk in it.

In 1949, the Roosevelt Hotel in New Orleans contested the use of the "Ramos gin fizz" name, so the Cadillac changed it on the menu to the New Orleans fizz. No matter. Everybody still ordered a Ramos.

The fanciest drink, a zombie, was the most expensive: $1 in 1955. Most other cocktails ranged from 40 to 80 cents.

Each morning, hundreds of pounds of block ice was delivered and stacked on wooden slats in the cooler until the bar crew arrived to start loading it into a hand-operated grinder. While the mechanics of the ice-grinding operation evolved over the years, until the day Porter left the Cadillac, it was all done on the premises, in the same cooler that was restored after the 1954 flood.

Porter: *Mayo was successful even though people told him nobody would come to Mexico and drink those fancy mixed drinks. But hell, he set them on their ear, and they loved it. I had to sneak margaritas on the menu because Mayo didn't believe much in changing things. He didn't think anybody would want to drink those newfangled things.*

We got the recipe from our old friend Margaret Sames, who invented the margarita during the Christmas holidays in 1948 at her vacation home in Acapulco.

Margaret's husband Bill ran the Ford dealership in Alice and his brother Harry ran the one in Laredo. They were the first Ford dealerships in Texas.

Growing up, I knew the word Cajun as a nickname for people who lived in southern Louisiana, around my grandparents' stomping grounds in Lafayette, New Iberia, and Abbeville. If America in the 1950s knew the word at all, it was from the cornball comedy of Justin Wilson, who was a celebrity Cajun long before Paul Prudhomme started blackening anything that moved.

The food at my great-grandfather Clay Savoie's table was smothered, sautéed, stuffed, and sauced. Nearly every savory dish relied on bell pepper, celery, and onion, the holy trinity of Louisiana cooking, but Cajun was never in the recipe title. Of course every cook in our family knew that "first, you start with a roux."

When Mayo put his South Louisiana friends to work in the kitchen, it was New Orleans meets New Laredo, his standard way of referring to Nuevo Laredo. He acquired a taste for turtle soup during his years in New Orleans, working at the St. Charles Hotel and Galatoire's.

Amos Graves, a doctor from San Antonio, was also in the oil business and had holdings around Freer and Mirando City. Any time he got within fifty miles of Laredo, he would come to the Cadillac and take home a gallon of turtle soup.

The Recipes

⪢ CABRITO ⪜
Serves 8

Baby goat was my sister Clay's favorite dish at the Cadillac. "*Para chuparse los dedos,*" she would say. At her birthday parties at the Cadillac, she and her friends might indeed lick their fingers after the meal.

Try to use a cabrito that weighs between 7½ and 8½ pounds, dressed. The tenderest cabrito will be about a month old and unweaned. Once they begin to eat grass, they get tough and develop a stronger, more mutton-like flavor. Marcus Wormser loved the Cadillac's cabrito. My father said he couldn't remember Marcus ever ordering anything else.

Have the butcher split the cabrito in half lengthwise. Place it in a heavy roasting pan. Rub it with cooking oil or a light olive

Porter made sure Clay got a prime table for her eighteenth birthday party in 1972. Celebrating with her are pals Frances Meyer, Micki Bruni, Laura Miranda, Laura Casso, and Clay.

oil and sprinkle liberally with salt and black pepper. In the roasting pan, place more oil, lard, or vegetable shortening and two or three onions, cut into chunks.

Preheat the over to 375°F. Bake for about 1½ hours, or until tender. After the cabrito has been cooking for about 30 minutes, baste it with 1 cup of hot olive oil. That crisps it up and helps seal the juices in. Continue to baste occasionally with the pan juices. It's ready when the skin is golden brown and crispy.

⇾ CHICKEN GUACAMOLE ⇽
Serves 4

This dish starts with basic guacamole and adds shredded strips of seasoned baked breast of chicken. It's a favorite party dish served with tostados or warm, crusty bolillos.

> 4 chicken breasts (split breasts with rib meat)
> Salt and finely ground fresh black pepper to taste
> Olive oil
> 12 avocados, preferably the black, pebble-skinned Hass
>   variety for the best flavor
> 2 to 3 small Mexican limes
> 1 teaspoon salt
> ⅛ teaspoon garlic powder
> ¼ cup finely chopped onion
> 1 cup chopped tomato

Season the chicken with salt and pepper, rub with oil, and bake in a 350°F oven until done. Remove from oven, cool, debone, and then shred the breasts into irregular pieces.

Halve the avocados, retaining at least one seed. With a spoon, scoop out the pulp. Squeeze the lime juice over the pulp and mash it with a fork or potato masher. Add 1 teaspoon salt and the garlic powder and blend well. Add the onion and tomatoes and blend again. Check for saltiness. Avocados require a lot of salt.

Mix in the shredded chicken and stir. Chill and serve.

December 2, 1979, our last Sunday lunch at the Cadillac. We enjoyed a family-style chicken guacamole lunch. Shown here are Wanda, Porter, and Suzy Mayo.

⇒ WINE SAUCE ⇐

Wine sauce is one of the dishes my family regards as a main dish as much as an accompaniment. Whenever my father made this at home, it was a daylong production, with everybody conscripted as galley crew. The heady aroma of beef, wine, and vegetables made us so hungry that we usually didn't wait for the filet or quail or chicken livers the sauce was intended for. All of us were guilty of dipping into the rich concoction with a tablespoon or sopping it up with bolillos. But try to wait, because as good as it is from a spoon, it's indescribably wonderful ladled over grilled quail.

Do make sure you have at least a 10-gallon pot and help in the kitchen. Obviously, this recipe makes more wine sauce than you'll use in one meal—unless you're cooking for the A&M track and field team after the Border Olympics.

If you persevere and cook this quantity, it freezes well and keeps a long time if you seal the containers carefully. But if this sounds like more chopping, dicing, and quartering than you'd care to devote a couple of days to, cut the recipe in half. Don't reduce it more than that, however, because the proportions won't work.

1 7-pound bone-in beef roast*
2 tablespoons flour
¼ cup olive oil
12 pounds onions, peeled and quartered
12 pounds ripe tomatoes
54 ounces tomato paste
10 ounces Lea & Perrins worchestershire sauce
10 ounces paprika
10 ounces (1½ cups) granulated sugar
3 tablespoons salt
1½ tablespoons black pepper
1 teaspoon allspice
1 teaspoon thyme
1 teaspoon cloves
2 heads garlic, peeled
16 ounces claret, Burgundy, or Chianti

Dust the beef with flour. Heat the olive oil in a large pot over medium-high heat. Add the beef and brown it on all sides. When it is golden brown, add about ½ cup water. Add all the remaining ingredients except the garlic and wine and stir.

Cover with water almost to the top of the pot.

Add the garlic. (No need to cut the garlic.)

Heat should be high enough to raise a low boil. Do not let it boil over.

Put the lid on and cook over low heat for 4 hours, stirring every 15 minutes. Lift the beef out and set aside. Strain the stock through a china cap, mashing the vegetables through the sides. Return the stock to the stove and simmer over low heat, uncovered, about 2 hours, or until the original volume is reduced by half. After 1 hour, add half the wine. When the sauce has reached the desired consistency, add the rest of the wine and cook for an additional 15 minutes.

Remove from the stove and refrigerate or freeze in meal-sized containers. When you're ready to serve, add about 1 ounce of wine for each cup of sauce and heat the sauce thoroughly.

Use the beef for tacos or sandwiches.

*Bone-in roasts are a rarity these days unless you have a butcher on the payroll. The Cadillac used the neck or head of the strip of meat that filet mignon is cut from.

⩔ NACHOS ⩗

My father's friend George O. Jackson Sr. was a big nacho eater, but very particular about how the cook fixed them. He'd go into the kitchen and tell the cook he wanted cheese on each tostada, one slice of jalapeno on each. Eventually the waiters knew how he wanted it. George's friend Sid Cunningham from San Antonio always had nachos and tequila sours.

Classic nachos start with home-fried tortilla chips or totopos, although store-bought chips can substitute. Use a cheese that melts consistently. The Cadillac always used Kraft American processed cheese in the blue cardboard box (a 5-pound loaf). Cheddar does *not* work.

To fry your own chips, use white corn tortillas cut into

The Garner girls typically celebrated their birthdays at the Cadillac. The author, seated in the middle, observes her tenth with friends Tina Gault, Connie Kowis, Elizabeth Link, Clay, and Lynn Powell. Standing are Laura Richards, Grace Gault, and Winnie Richards.

quarters. Fry the tortillas in hot oil until golden brown. Drain in a paper sack and salt the chips while they're hot.

Grate cheese thinly and mound on each chip individually. Top with cross-section slices of pickled jalapeño peppers. Arrange the nachos on an ovenproof dish and place under the broiler until the cheese melts and becomes bubbly. Hot plate!

For a variation, the Cadillac sometimes added small chunks of tender grilled sirloin before putting the chips under the broiler and then garnished each nacho with a dollop of guacamole.

At my birthday parties, guests arrived to find platters of nachos on the table. They remain my favorite indulgence.

⇛ CRABMEAT NEWBURG ⇚
6 servings

Mayo liked to serve this dish over toast points. It's also very good over steamed white rice. (But of course in this family, *everything's* good with white rice.)

> 2 pounds lump crabmeat
> Salt and freshly ground black pepper to taste
> Cayenne to taste
> 4 tablespoons butter
> ½ cup dry sherry (not cooking sherry)
> ½ cup heavy cream
> Yolks of 4 hard-boiled eggs, minced
> 4 sprigs of fresh parsley, chopped

Season the flaked crabmeat with salt, pepper, and cayenne. In a saucepan over low heat, melt butter, taking care not to scorch it. Add the crab and sherry and simmer gently. In another pan over low heat, warm the cream and minced egg yolks. Watch that it doesn't boil.

Stir the crab into the cream-egg mixture and heat gently. Spoon into four ramekins and set them under the broiler for 2 to 3 minutes. Sprinkle chopped parsley on top of each dish and serve.

❧ BEEF TACOS *SUAVES* ❧
(Soft Corn Tortillas)
12 tortillas

2 pounds lean ground beef
¼ cup finely chopped onion
Salt
1 tablespoon ground cumin
2 fresh serrano peppers, split lengthwise
1 head iceberg lettuce, chopped
5 tomatoes, chopped
¼ cup vinaigrette
12 white corn tortillas
2 avocados, sliced (optional)
Cheddar cheese, grated (optional)
1 avocado, peeled, pitted, and sliced (optional)
Oil for cooking

There are several steps to this dish, but don't be daunted. The results are worth the effort. In a heavy skillet over medium heat, brown the ground beef and onions, seasoning liberally with salt and cumin. Drain the oil as the meat browns, adding more cumin to taste. Once the meat browns, add the serranos. Cover the pan and simmer for about 10 minutes.

In a salad bowl, toss the lettuce and tomatoes with the vinaigrette.

Heat the tortillas with a little grease on a comal or in a skillet.

Put a couple of spoonfuls of beef into the tortillas, but don't make them too fat. Fold each tortilla in half and secure with toothpicks. Cook until they hold their shape but just before they start to get crisp. Drain on paper towels. Sprinkle with salt if desired.

Remove the toothpicks and add the lettuce and tomato mixture. Garnish with cheese and slices of avocado if desired.

Can be messy, but boy, are they good!

⇒ ITALIAN SALAD ⇐
8 servings

Two salads on the menu carried names that are now considered derogatory terms for Italian Americans, but when Mayo was working in New Orleans, they were popular choices at most of the white tablecloth restaurants in New Orleans. The salads were served on chilled plates and were showy and fun, with boiled shrimp, anchovies, and asparagus crisscrossed atop the mounded lettuce.

For the Dressing
 ¾ cup olive oil
 ¼ cup red wine vinegar
 1 tablespoon Italian seasoning
 1 tablespoon Lea & Perrins worchestershire sauce

For the Salad
Three heads of lettuce torn into bite-sized pieces: romaine, iceberg, and butter (Bibb)

 1½ to 2 cups olive salad*
 2 tomatoes, cut into wedges
 6 to 8 cloves garlic, minced
 16 flat anchovies, packed in oil
 8 extra-large shrimp, boiled in the shell, then peeled and chilled
 8 asparagus spears, steamed and chilled (large spears hold
     up better)
 Shaved fresh Parmesan cheese

In a small bowl, whisk together all the ingredients for the dressing. In a large bowl, combine the lettuce, olive salad, tomatoes, and dressing and toss well to coat the lettuce evenly. Distribute salad evenly on eight chilled salad plates. Top each mound of lettuce with crisscrossed anchovies, a shrimp, and an asparagus spear. Finish with Parmesan shavings.

*This recipe relies on a redolent olive salad base, using a long list of ingredients that will have you chopping for half a day before marinating it overnight. The Cadillac cooks concocted the olive salad by the quart, but I stock up on jars at Central Grocery whenever I'm in New Orleans. Several ready-made brands are available at specialty stores or online and the internet also has recipes, if you're feeling industrious.

⇒ SHRIMP À LA LOUISIANE ⬿
1 quart dressing for 2 pounds shrimp

Patsy Martin Galo teases me that I must have omitted something from this recipe because her attempts at this sauce never taste like the Cadillac version. It's sad but true: nothing ever tasted so good as when it came out of the Cadillac kitchen.

    4 cups mayonnaise
    2 tablespoons ketchup
    1 heaping teaspoon Creole mustard
    ½ teaspoon paprika
    1 teaspoon lemon juice
    3 to 4 drops Tabasco sauce
    ¼ cup minced parsley

Mix ingredients, tasting and adjusting as necessary. Store in tightly sealed container. Serve over cold boiled shrimp atop a bed of shredded lettuce.

⇒ PICO DE GALLO OR SALSA CRUDA ⬿
2 cups pico de gallo

Long before America took chips and hot sauce for granted at Mexican restaurants, the Cadillac had its own standard gustatory greeting. Waiters delivered a basket of bolillos and saltine crackers and a bowl of this hot sauce to your table while you were still scooting your chairs closer in.

My grandfather emptied two or three servings during a meal. His favorite approach was to scoop out the center of a bolillo and fill the crusty bread with spoons full of the salsa and sometimes with guacamole. At the end of a meal, Mayo had an array of balls of the bread itself next to his plate.

When the parking lot zoo still existed, he would let me feed the bolillo leftovers to whatever critter I favored.

4 very ripe medium tomatoes, unpeeled, finely chopped
    (Roma or plum tomatoes are best)
1 white onion, finely chopped
9 serrano chiles, minced
8 to 10 cilantro leaves, chopped
Juice of 1 lime
Salt

Mix the tomatoes, serranos, and cilantro, mashing slightly. Use a large molcajete if you have one. Add lime juice and salt to taste. If you prefer a smoother, more homogenous salsa, you can puree it in a blender or food processor.

⇥ CHICKEN ENVUELTOS ⇤
Makes 4 servings (3 tortillas per serving)

This was a favorite dish of Pat Knight, my father's friend from San Antonio. After a professional football career, Knight owned Allen & Allen Company and was a partner in the "Camp Had It" hunting lodge in Webb County.

1 pound shredded cooked chicken
2 medium white onions
4 cloves garlic, minced
1 green bell pepper, julienned
1 serrano chile, seeded and chopped (more to your taste)
1 (15-ounce) can tomatoes
3 chicken bouillon cubes, dissolved in water
2 tablespoons ground cumin
Salt and freshly ground black pepper to taste

1 dozen thin white corn tortillas
Finely shredded cheddar cheese
Oil for cooking

Finely chop one onion. Cut second onion in quarters and separate the sections and set aside.

Put a little oil in large sauté pan or skillet and add the garlic, the bell pepper, and about a third of the chopped onion. Add serrano and tomatoes. Stir well, breaking up tomatoes. Let it stew a while and blend together. Add bouillon mixture.

Add cumin, salt, and pepper to taste. Cook 4 to 5 minutes over medium heat. Add chicken and remaining onion and enough hot water to cover. Cook for about 20 minutes.

Make individual servings: lay a tortilla on plate. Cover with a small amount of the remaining chopped onion, the cheese, and a spoonful of chicken mixture. Roll tortilla. Repeat. Garnish with more chopped onion and an ample amount of chicken mixture and cheese.

Put plate at a time in the microwave to melt the cheese slightly.

Two Ways to Prepare Tortillas

1. The old way: Dip the tortillas in the chicken mixture to soften.

2. The new way: Lay a couple of tortillas on paper towels and sprinkle with a little water. Make additional layers. Heat in the microwave until just softened. (Dad preferred this method because the tortillas don't tear and you won't lose your religion trying to roll them.)

⇒ TURTLE SOUP ⇐
Serves 6 to 8

1 to 1½ pounds turtle meat,* thawed and put through a grinder or food processor

½ cup olive oil
2 ribs celery, coarsely chopped
1 large onion, coarsely chopped
½ bell pepper, coarsely chopped
1 cup flour
Cayenne pepper
1 tablespoon salt
Freshly ground black pepper
2 quarts beef stock
½ cup tomato paste
1 tablespoon minced garlic
2 teaspoons mace
2 teaspoons Tabasco sauce
1½ teaspoons lemon juice
½ cup dry sherry (do not use cooking sherry)
2 hard-boiled eggs, finely chopped or sieved
½ cup finely chopped parsley

Use a heavy pot (cast iron is good) large enough to hold 4 to 5 quarts. Sauté the turtle meat in the olive oil until very brown, stirring to break it up. Stir in the celery, onion, and bell pepper and cook until they are translucent. Add the flour and stir to blend well.

Add cayenne, salt, and pepper to taste.

Slowly add the stock and stir continuously as the mixture thickens. Stir in the tomato paste. Let it simmer over low heat for about 20 minutes.

Then add the garlic, mace, Tabasco, lemon juice, and sherry. Cook for another 30 minutes. Just before serving, add the sieved hard-boiled eggs and parsley.

Optional: Each bowl of soup can be served with a shot of sherry on the side.

*Turtle meat is a farmed, sustainable product, available frozen in specialty food stores or by mail order on the Internet. Please avoid the canned version.

⇛ NEW IBERIA SHRIMP GUMBO ⇚

4 to 6 servings

Shrimp gumbo was never on the menu at the Cadillac, but this family favorite was among my grandmother Odette's best dishes. Today my youngest son, Cooper, keeps a culinary calendar according to "gumbo season," recalling family lore that it was too hot in Texas to cook gumbo before Halloween.

Part of the Cajun ritual is to downplay compliments, borne out by our own family's ritual.

"The gumbo is wonderful, Mamo," we'd coo to my grandmother. Her chest would swell, and she would smile, shaking her head, saying, "I don't know. I think the roux is a little off this time."

Her demurral was our cue to go overboard with the compliments for the gumbo, which of course was always perfect, always the best we'd ever eaten.

2 pounds of shrimp
Salt and freshly ground pepper
Cayenne pepper
3 stalks celery, chopped (to make 1 cup), with leaves set aside
1 teaspoon black peppercorns
⅔ cup flour
¾ cup oil (regular cooking oil is best; don't use olive oil)
1 cup chopped white onion
1 cup chopped green bell pepper
6 green onions, chopped
Filé powder (ground sassafras)
Tabasco sauce

Peel and devein the shrimp. Season them generously with salt, pepper, and cayenne and set aside.

Put the shrimp shells in a large stockpot with the celery leaves, black peppercorns, and 2 to 3 quarts of water. Bring to a boil. Once the shells have boiled, lower the heat and keep the stock simmering while you make the roux.

In a heavy pot (I use a cast-iron Dutch oven), stir the flour into the oil. Keep stirring until the roux slowly browns. It's a long process, but worth the dark richness. Once the roux reaches a chocolatey color, remove the pot from the heat source and immediately add the onion, 1 cup chopped celery, and bell pepper to lower the temperature and keep the roux from scorching. Stir to coat the vegetables with the roux, then add the shrimp and stir until all ingredients are thoroughly mixed and coated with roux.

Strain out the shells and add the hot stock to the gumbo pot. Stir to blend well and cook on low heat for about an hour. Add more salt, pepper, and cayenne to taste.

Add the green onions about 10 minutes before serving. Serve over white rice, with filé and Tabasco on the side.

⇥ ONIONS AND KETCHUP ⇤

My father's dear friend Jim Mayo always ordered the same thing: shrimp cocktail, wop salad, and a filet. The bus boy brought bolillos and a mound of chopped onions—at least a whole onion. While Jim waited for the main course, he'd dig the middle out of the bolillos and fill it with onions and ketchup. That was his appetizer. Then he would fill up his shrimp cocktail with the onions, stir, and eat. He'd cover his salad with more onions and cover all of that with ketchup. When his food came, he'd take the rest of the onions, make a peak on top of the steak, and empty the ketchup bottle over all.

⇉ BOLILLOS ⋞
Makes 8 bolillos

Thanks to Cadillac devotee Ernie Stromberger of Austin for sharing this recipe.

    ½ cup sourdough starter
    1 cup milk
    2 cups unbleached all-purpose flour (divided)
    ¾ teaspoon salt
    2 teaspoons sugar
    Pinch ground cinnamon
    1 teaspoon baking powder
    ½ teaspoon baking soda
    ½ cup cake flour
    1 cup water plus 1 teaspoon salt for misting

Follow any recipe for sourdough starter 8 to 12 hours before you
    need the bolillos.
In a large bowl, mix together: sourdough starter, milk, and 1 cup
    of the all-purpose flour.
Cover bowl and keep at room temperature. When ready to make
    bolillos, stir in the second cup of flour. Combine salt, sugar,
    cinnamon, baking powder, and baking soda with ½ cup cake
    flour and sift over the top of the dough.
Mix well by hand. Knead on a lightly floured board.
Cut dough in half, rolling each half into log. Cut each log into
    four equal pieces, shaping each into a torpedo, forcing nar-
    row ends and a fat middle. Let set in a warm place to rise for
    about 30 minutes, preferably in a bounded-bottom baguette
    baking pan.
Heat oven (convection preferred) to 500°F with baking stone if
    baguette pans are not being used.
Slash rolls lengthwise with a razor and mist with salt water. Put in
    oven in baguette pan or on baking stone.
Reduce oven heat to 400° and cook 20 minutes or until internal
    heat registers 210°F.

⇒ PAN-ROASTED CHACHALACA WITH BLACK SAUCE ⇐
Serves 4

Chachalacas, also known as Mexican tree pheasants, are large birds found in South Texas, the Rio Grande Valley, and northern Mexico. Dad said any time he could find chachalaca, he would get on the telephone and fill the Cadillac.

"If I didn't let certain customers know I had them, they'd be unhappy," he said. "The Longoria family especially loved the dish."

If you don't have a friend who can supply chachalacas, substitute a plump chicken hen. One word of caution, though: If you don't like liver, you're certainly not going to like this sauce.

Chachalaca
> 1 chachalaca, cut into serving pieces as for fried chicken
> Salt and freshly ground black pepper to taste
> 3 tablespoons flour
> 2 bacon slices, chopped
> 1 yellow onion, thinly sliced
> 1 cup dry white wine

Season the chachalaca with salt and pepper and dust lightly with flour. In a large cast -iron saucepan, sauté the bacon until it is crisp and brown. Add the chachalaca pieces and turn frequently. When they are browned, add the onions and wine and bring to a boil. Cover the pan, reduce the heat, and simmer for 30 to 40 minutes, or until tender. Remove the chachalaca to a warm platter while you make the sauce. Save the pan drippings for the sauce.

Black Sauce
Enough sauce for 1 bird
> 1 liver (Substitute goose liver if the chachalaca comes
> already cleaned)
> ¼ teaspoon ground anise
> ¼ teaspoon ground ginger
> ¼ teaspoon ground cinnamon
> ¼ cup bread crumbs

½ teaspoon kosher salt
2 teaspoons verjus*
1 cup pan drippings (and/or chicken stock)
¼ cup red wine (optional)

Sauté the liver until it is well cooked but not dried out. Combine with the other ingredients except the pan drippings or stock and puree until smooth. Add the pan drippings or stock and simmer the mixture for about 10 minutes. Add wine if desired. Pour the sauce over the chachalaca and serve.

*Verjus is a sour juice from unripened grapes that's available in specialty stores or online. You can substitute lemon juice or white wine vinegar.

⇒ NEW ORLEANS GIN FIZZ ⇐
Serves 1

WARNING: these sweet concoctions pack an unsuspecting punch and can be lethal on a hot summer day. Customers at the Cadillac would wander in from the July heat, toss back two or three of these, and then wilt on the street when they went back outside.

1 tablespoon confectioners' sugar (sifted)
1 ounce gin
2 ounces cold milk
10 drops orange flower water*
Juice of one lime
1 egg white
Ice

Mix ingredients in order. Shake in a cocktail shaker until you think your arms will surely drop off. Strain. Serve. Mix up more.

*The orange flower water is hard to find, but absolutely essential to the allure of this drink. Find it in specialty liquor stores or order it online.

⇒ TOM & JERRY ⇐
12 to 15 servings

At Christmastime, my grandfather and later my father would bring the big porcelain punch bowl out and mix up a batch of Tom & Jerry batter. The Tom & Jerry was a sweet drink, kind of a hot eggnog served in coffee mugs.

When company came over, Big Daddy would ladle the batter into his special Tom & Jerry mugs, add the liquor, and fill the mug with boiling water. Ever the bartender, he would stir with professional flourish and sprinkle the top with nutmeg.

And although we children were allowed a sip or two, the grown-ups were quick to reclaim the mugs before we got walloped by the bourbon and rum that give the drink its punch.

12 eggs, separated
4 cups granulated sugar
2 to 3 ounces dark, heavy rum or a fruit brandy

To make the batter, in a medium bowl add the sugar a little at a time to the beaten egg yolks until well blended. Add sufficient sugar to make the batter very thick.

In a separate bowl, beat the egg whites. Then slowly add about three-fourths of the beaten egg whites to the sugar mixture. As it gets easier to stir, add a little more sugar, then the rest of the egg whites.

Test the consistency of the batter by dripping it from a wooden spoon. The batter should drip very slowly.

Then add the liquor. Add more sugar if it gets too thin. Don't be afraid to add too much sugar.

To serve, stir the batter well. Then put 1 tablespoon of the batter into a hot mug, add 1 ounce of bourbon, and fill the mug with boiling water. Stir until well mixed. Sprinkle with nutmeg if you like and serve. If the batter gets a little sugary after a couple of days, just give it a good stir.

Afterword

When we were children and into middle adulthood, my Laredo friends and I crossed the Rio Grande into Nuevo Laredo as though we were walking across a street in our neighborhood. No thoughts of danger, no fears beyond being caught with a smuggled bottle of Bacardi we didn't want to pay duty on.

The river was not a boundary it was just geography. The people in Nuevo Laredo, the merchants, the artists and musicians were our classmates, our friends, our family. Anyone born and reared in los dos Laredos will tell you that growing up on the border nurtured us in a porous cultural paradise of shared rich heritages. We endured the poverty, the unpaved streets, and the heat. We bought *elote* from a cart and fresh flowers and *chanclas* (flip-flops) at the mercado. We were one people, living on two sides of a river.

Today, venturing across that river is strictly business, a quick trip to a doctor or a butcher shop. The tourists who are driving to interior locales like Monterrey or San Miguel de Allende do so in haste—no lingering lunches in Nuevo Laredo, no Ramos gin fizzes.

The US Department of State continues to urge increased caution in Mexico due to crime, specifically advising American citizens to avoid Nuevo Laredo and the state of Tamaulipas due to violent crime. The department's website notes that gang activity, including gun battles, is widespread in Nuevo Laredo and Piedras Negras. Gunfights generally occur after dark, but there have been some in broad daylight, on public streets, and close to public venues. While the State Department notes that the vast majority of victims have been gang members and law enforcement fighting them, innocent bystanders also have died in the shootouts.

Nuevo Laredo does not have a municipal police force. State and federal police forces have assumed law enforcement duties, aided by the Mexican army and Marines.

The year 2018 was especially violent in Nuevo Laredo. The *Laredo Morning Times* reported deadly shootouts between drug traffickers and the Mexican military that claimed the lives of bystanders and children, while journalists and political figures were viciously murdered.

The *Laredo Morning Times* said one of the most notable incidents occurred in July 2018, when suspected hit men affiliated with the Cártel del Noreste exchanged gunfire with troops outside of a popular Nuevo Laredo mall. The incident was caught on video and shared extensively on Facebook. The shootout came just two days after the city's prison director was shot dead on the street.

On the American side of the border, Laredo also had a particularly violent 2018, making national headlines with several gruesome crimes more related to sexual assault and murder than to drug cartel activity.

Overall, though, Laredo continues to be a safe place to live and raise a family. Crime dropped significantly between 2009 and 2018. Homicide cases declined by 36 percent, while robbery decreased 47 percent, and aggravated assault was down 30 percent, according to the Laredo police department's annual report.

In the spring of 2019, Laredo once again attracted global scrutiny. This time the coverage was positive, with the visits of two luminaries who brought messages of peace and unity, shaded by political controversy over the immigration crisis and the border wall.

US Speaker of the House Nancy Pelosi came to Laredo in February 2019 and attended several events connected to the annual Washington Birthday Celebration that weekend, including the Caballeros Cocktail Party before the Society of Martha Washington's Colonial Pageant and the annual *abrazo* ceremony Saturday morning in the middle of the Juarez-Lincoln Bridge.

Writing in the *San Antonio Express-News*, columnist Elaine Ayala reported that four days earlier, Pelosi had left Washington, DC, the city where President Trump declared that the US-Mexico border was a national emergency, citing "imaginary statistics of violence so severe he insisted it required access to the Pentagon's budget to secure the border with a wall." Ayala said that

US Speaker of the House Nancy Pelosi attended several events connected to the 2019 Washington's Birthday Celebration, including the
abrazo ceremony in the middle of the Juárez-Lincoln International
Bridge. Shown here are Patty Bruni, US Representative Henry Cuellar
(D-Laredo), Pelosi, and Ernest M. "Rocky" Bruni, who portrayed George
Washington in the 122nd annual celebration. Photo from the collection
of Rocky Bruni.

on Saturday morning, Pelosi "arrived at a border town that had
no such national emergency but was steeped in an all-American
celebration in honor of the first American president and beloved
founding father."

The traditional bridge ceremony honors the international ties
between Laredo and Nuevo Laredo, Tamaulipas and Texas, Mexico and the United States. In a public display of goodwill, Pelosi
exchanged an *abrazo* with Francisco García Cabeza de Vaca, governor of Tamaulipas.

A couple of months later, world-renowned cellist Yo-Yo Ma
visited los dos Laredos as part of his international Bach Project,

Cellist Yo-Yo Ma visited Laredo in April 2019 as part of his Bach Project. During this Day of Action, Ma brought a message of cultural unity, saying, "We build bridges, not walls." Photo taken by Armando X. Lopez of Laredo.

a two-year initiative to play all six Bach cello suites in thirty-six cities on six continents. Ma said he aimed to use Bach's music to explore connections between two cultures. On a cool April morning, Ma took the stage in a park on the riverbank in the shadow of the same bridge that hosts the international *abrazos*.

Before he took up his bow, Ma said, "We are a country, not a hotel, and we are not full. In culture, we seek truth and understanding. In culture, we build bridges, not walls."

Ma's Day of Action also included private meetings with leaders in Nuevo Laredo and in Laredo, a concert in Plaza Juárez in Nuevo Laredo, and a performance with the Laredo Philharmonic Orchestra.

Hugh Fitzsimons, a third-generation rancher in Dimmitt County in South Texas, attended the public and private events in Laredo and interviewed Ma. Writing in *Texas Monthly* online, Fitzsimons said Ma emphasized the point that people must "celebrate what we have in common, then pass it on." Fitzsimons said the river is really a border in name only.

True that. The Rio Grande is just geography, something Laredoans and Nuevo Laredoans never gave a second thought to for more than two centuries.

Ay te watcho.

Timeline

1745: Explorer Jacinto de León identifies Laredo as a crossing
point for the Rio Grande.

1883: A permanent railroad bridge is built across the Rio Grande.

1885: Achille Mehault "Mayo" Bessan is born in New Iberia, Louisiana.

1889: The Texas Mexican Railway runs trains from Canada to
Mexico City, establishing Laredo's future as the busiest land
port in the United States.

1903: Mayo Bessan moves to New Orleans, where he played
poker and tended bar in several of the city's more than 5,000
watering holes.

1910–1920: The Mexican Revolution thrusts Mexico into cultural
and political upheaval.

1914–1918: Nuevo Laredo property is devastated, and the central
business district destroyed by revolutionary fighting.

1915: Jelly Roll Morton writes the "Jelly Roll Blues."

1917: The United States joins allies Britain, France, and Russia to
fight World War I.

1918: "Rum-running" becomes a thriving business in Louisiana
and Texas after Congress ratifies the Eighteenth Amend-
ment.

1919: Between mid-December and mid-January 1920, 99,991 gallons of whiskey and 1.3 million gallons of alcohol sailed out
of the Port of New Orleans, headed mainly for South America.

1920: Prohibition becomes the law of the land. Henry C. Ramos
closed his bar at 712 Gravier Street and Mayo is out of a job.
Stabbed in a fight, Mayo leaves New Orleans and returns to

New Iberia. Recovering from surgery, he opens a newsstand and runs high-stakes poker games in a back room.

1920: Pancho Villa (José Doroteo Arango Arámbula) agreed to end his active fighting in the Mexican Revolution, and retired to a hacienda in Chihuahua, given to him by the government.

1921: Oklahoma wildcatter O. W. Killam brings in the first commercial oil well and launches the South Texas oil boom, thirty miles east of Laredo.

1923: Pancho Villa is assassinated July 20 while driving near his home in Parral, Chihuahua, likely with the approval of Álvaro Obregón, then president of Mexico.

1923: Mayo Bessan, thirty-eight, marries Odette Savoie, eighteen. On their honeymoon in San Antonio, he leaves his bride with a cousin and heads to Nuevo Laredo, Mexico, to scout out the business possibilities.

1924: Mayo and Odette move to Nuevo Laredo, where he leased a bar on the main street, Calle Guerrero, and called it the Cadillac, because he thought the name sounded rich.

1924: Don Octaviano Longoria moves from groceries to beer, becoming the Cuauhtémoc distributor and eventually building Nuevo Laredo's first ice plant.

1926: Wanda Bessan, Odette and Mayo's only child, is born. A few months later, the family moves across the Rio Grande from Nuevo Laredo to Laredo.

1929: Mexico's long-dominant political party, the Partido Nacional Revolucionario (PNR), is founded.

1929: Pan-American Highway construction from Mexico City finally begins in Nuevo Laredo. Mexico forbids alcohol sales within ten meters of the highway. Mayo rents a bar two blocks away and opens the "big" Cadillac Bar.

1929: The Great Depression begins.

1930: Operations begin in North Laredo at what will become Texas Mining & Smelting, one of the world's largest antimony smelters.

1932: Mayo buys out his partner Pete Coussoulis, who ran the Cadillac's kitchen.

1936: The 749-mile stretch of the Pan-American Highway between Nuevo Laredo and Mexico City is completed.

1940: A modern four-lane Gateway to the Americas bridge opens between Laredo and Nuevo Laredo.

1941: The United States enters World War II after Japan bombs Pearl Harbor.

1942: Don Octaviano Longoria's son, "Chito" Longoria, begins exporting bar soap to the United States. He names the soap after his daughter, Gloria.

1942: Laredo Army Air Field and gunnery range opens on 2,000 acres north of town on US Highway 59.

1942: Planning begins for the US food-rationing program. Many Laredoans begin getting groceries in Nuevo Laredo.

1945: On April 11, 2nd Lt. Porter Garner is seriously wounded in Germany. He spends almost ten months in hospitals in England, Michigan, and Louisiana, much of that time in a full body cast.

1946: Porter Garner marries Wanda Bessan.

1947: Porter joins his father-in-law, Mayo, at the Cadillac Bar.

1947: The Art Deco Plaza Theatre opens, built by H. B. Zachry, a Laredo native who ultimately owned one of the world's largest construction companies.

1951: Waiters, cooks, and bartenders go on strike at the Cadillac and throughout Nuevo Laredo, demanding double pay for US holidays, including Independence Day and Washington's Birthday.

1952: The old army airfield is reactivated as Laredo Air Force Base for basic flight training, bringing an influx of new residents to the city.

1953: Drought causes the Rio Grande to stop flowing. It was dry enough to walk across the riverbed in Laredo.

1954: Mexico devalues the peso, from 8.64 pesos to the dollar to 12.4 to the dollar.

1954: In April, construction of the Falcon Dam and reservoir on the Rio Grande is completed, forty miles southeast of Laredo near Zapata, Texas.

1954: On June 10, the Eisenhower administration launches "Operation Wetback." Starting in California and moving to Texas, the Border Patrol rounded up and deported an estimated 1 million Mexicans.

1954: On June 24, Hurricane Alice makes landfall at Brownsville, Texas, eventually dumping 38 inches of rain on the Devils River–Pecos Divide in the Texas Hill Country.

1954: On June 30, the Rio Grande crests at 65.35 feet, about 15 feet above the Laredo International Bridge.

1955: On April 1, the Cadillac Bar reopens, with central air conditioning.

1965: Lyndon Johnson declares a "war on poverty," identifies Laredo as the poorest city in America.

1965: Customs officials at the Laredo Bridge arrest Timothy Leary and two children and charged them with illegal possession of marijuana after finding a "roach" in the car and marijuana concealed in the underwear of his seventeen-year-old, Susan. Laredo attorneys John Fitzgibbon and Tom Goodwin represented Leary, and Chuck Fansler represented Leary's daughter.

1969: On September 8, Amistad Dam is completed in Del Rio, Texas, 179 miles northwest of Laredo. President Richard Nixon and Mexican president Gustavo Díaz Ordaz attend dedication.

1969: On September 21, vehicle inspections mandated by the Nixon administration's "Operation Intercept"—aimed at drug trafficking from Mexico—snarls traffic and causes hours of backup on the Laredo bridge. This depresses the economy in Laredo and Nuevo Laredo. The program is suspended in less than a month.

1969: On December 8, Mayo Bessan dies.

1973: The US government closes Laredo Air Force Base.

1976: Laredo's second bridge opens, with six lanes connecting directly to Interstate 35.

1977: George O. Jackson and partners open their version of the Cadillac Bar in Houston.

1979: On December 2, Porter gives the keys to the Cadillac to his
    employees and wishes them *buena suerte.*

2007: On July 29, Porter dies.

2010: On September 26, Wanda Bessan Garner dies.

Index